ALONE

GILLIAN WELLS

ALONE

GILLIAN WELLS

Gillian Wells
Visit my website at www.Gillianwellsauthor.com.au

Printed in Australia

First Printing: November 2020
Shawline Publishing Group Pty Ltd
www.shawlinepublishing.com.au

Paperback ISBN- 9781922444134

Ebook ISBN- 9781922444141

To Bill and Lynn Dahlheimer, who unknowingly inspired me to write this book.

Also, to Bradley Shaw for his help and encouragement and, of course, my amazing family for their support.

CHAPTER 1

Rachel woke with a start, her heart hammering in her chest. What had woken her? Was she dreaming or was it a noise? Dear old Nellie her faithful cattle dog slept outside her door on the veranda, but she was so deaf now she wouldn't hear anything. These thoughts tumbled through her head as she lay there trying to calm down. Then she heard the top step of the veranda steps creak, it had been doing that for some time when anyone stood on it. She sat bolt upright and looked at the luminous dial on the clock, 1.45 am. With racing heart, she slithered out of bed and crept to the door of her room. She stood listening but could hear nothing; cautiously she opened the bedroom door slowly. Not daring to put on the light, she tiptoed down the hallway and into Sam's little office. By feel, as it was so dark, she opened the gun cabinet and took out his old gun. Inevitably, she made a few small sounds and kept stopping to listen, but all seemed quiet. She was aware of a presence though or was it her imagination? Very slowly, she opened the front door.

No one there. *'Of course not'* she thought, she had been too long getting there. Smoke! She turned her head and could see a cigarette glowing in the dark to her right. Now feeling terrified, she swung the gun towards it just as a man's voice said, 'You want to be careful with that thing, Ma, you might do someone some harm.'

'Johnny?' Rachel lowered the gun. 'Is that you?' It was a rhetorical question of course; she knew his voice instantly. 'What do you want?'

'That's a question for your nearest and dearest, why would I want anything?'

Holding the gun by her side in one hand, Rachel turned and snapped on the veranda lights then turned back to her son.

He was unshaven, his curly blonde hair was down to his shoulders and he had a full beard, his grey eyes regarded his mother coldly as he towered over her, at six foot four he made Rachel feel small though she was average height.

'You only show up if you want something, you couldn't even be bothered to come to your father's funeral,' Rachel said bitterly.

'Old man got his just deserts in the end; anyway, he didn't care about me so I didn't care about him.'

Rachel flinched at his words but didn't reply. It was fruitless to argue she knew only too well, Johnny always said things that would hurt; she should be used to them by now she thought.

'Aren't you going to offer your son and heir a drink then, Ma?' Johnny finally said after several moments they had spent regarding each other with hostility.

Rachel hesitated then shrugged and turned back indoors, Johnny followed her as she retraced her steps down the hallway and into the kitchen.

'Tea or coffee?'

'I'd rather have something stronger, beer, whisky?'

'I haven't anything like that in the house, you either have tea or coffee or go, the choice is yours.'

Johnny slumped down at the kitchen table. 'Tea then.'

Rachel bustled about making the tea, her mind racing. Their only child: after a series of miscarriages, Rachel and Sam had doted on their son. He had been a delightful child, full of fun but loving and kind. Then one day he had a bad fall from his pony hitting his head. He was rushed to hospital by the Flying Doctor Service and for some time it didn't look good. The doctors feared brain damage, but when he finally came round, he seemed to be fine. Or was he? No damage in the normal sense but a personality change, a big one and no one had been able to help. Their ten-year-old son had become a monster over-night. He was feral, rude, abusive, disobedient, and ultimately destructive. Numerous professionals were engaged to help the family, but nothing seemed to be the answer. He would behave when he had to, but once he was home, he reverted. Finally aged fourteen, he grabbed a knife out of the knife block in the kitchen when rowing with his father. He lunged at Sam, who instinctively dodged while Rachel screamed at Johnny to stop.

2

Johnny threw the knife down and fled outside; he jumped in the ute and was gone. The ute was found abandoned in the nearest small town but no sign of Johnny. It was six years before they saw him again when he turned up wanting money. They had no spare cash and told him so. He stayed a few days and nothing in his behaviour was any better. It was worse if anything as he was now a strong man, taller than his father and there was an underlying menace in every word he uttered. Finally, Sam drove to the bank in town and drew five thousand dollars out giving it to his son on his return home. Johnny took it and left saying he would be back soon and would want more next time. His father would be dead before he returned, which he had done now.

Rachel sighed, she didn't like to admit it, but she was scared of him, she wouldn't, couldn't let it show, though. What did he want, he certainly wouldn't want to take over the farm? Ever since his accident he had total disinterest, all he seemed to be interested in was money. But what did he do with it? She looked at him again, he was dressed from head to toe in black leather. The penny dropped, he had become a bikie, at least he looked like one.

For some minutes, mother and son sat silently, both sipping the hot tea. Then Rachel took a big breath and said as calmly as she could, 'Are you here to stay, or do you want money or is it something else, why are you here?'

Johnny sat regarding his mother coldly for a heartbeat then drawled, 'Well, I heard the old man had finally kicked the bucket and I figured you wouldn't be staying so I came to claim my share before you buggered off with it all.'

'Sorry to disappoint you, but I intend to stay on for the time being at least,' Rachel spoke a lot more firmly than she felt.

'Is that so, Ma, I thought you might say that. Somehow though, I don't think you'll be here long, bit lonely out here without the old man. All sorts of things could happen, woman on her own, not so easy. A little place in town would suit you a lot better I'm thinking.'

'Are you threatening me, Johnny, is that what you came to do, take what you think is yours and then leave again? Don't you care at all about your dad, me, the farm, anything?' Even as she said all this Rachel knew the answer, but she had to say it anyway.

Johnny gave a snort of laughter. 'Why should I care, what did you ever do for me and that old bastard you say was my father? Well, good riddance is what I say. You owe me, Ma, I want what should be mine, sell this dump and give me what I want, and I will be only too pleased to stay away from you.'

As he uttered this last sentence, Johnny leaned forward and stared at his mother with cold hard eyes. Rachel flinched, there was hatred there lurking under the surface and his words cut her to the quick. She looked away unable to bear his gaze. Johnny got to his feet and on reaching the door said, 'Mind what I say, Ma, sell up and soon. I'll be back.' Then he was gone. Moments later, she heard a powerful motorbike roar away.

CHAPTER 2

The next morning, Rachel dragged herself out of bed. She had sat at the table in the kitchen for a long time after her son had left. Sometimes crying, sometimes consumed with anger, but in the end chilled and tired, she had gone back to her bed and to her surprise, she had slept. She still had a small nucleus of their original herd of stud cattle though she was gradually winding them down. It was now nine months since Sam had died. He had cancer, but he thought he had plenty of time to sell up and move, sort the business out, make provision for Rachel, all those things; but the cancer had other ideas, and he only lived a very short time after being diagnosed. That time had been taken up with fighting the illness and trying to make the most of the precious time he had left. The last few weeks when he realised that he was running out of time and that there was nothing more the doctors could do, he worried about the farm and Rachel. For her part, Rachel did her best to stem his fears saying she would cope, and it would all be fine. It wasn't of course, as the preceding years had seen a bad drought and although they had kept their head above water, it was only by the skin of their teeth. Rachel knew there would be taxes to pay and that she would have to make some provision for Johnny even in the circumstances they were in. Sam had left a small amount of money to Johnny because their lawyer said they must, but Rachel knew it wouldn't be enough. So, she had started to weed the less valuable cattle out and planned to wait and see the outcome of probate before she jumped in and sold everything up. Sam would have been heartbroken, she knew. She didn't know where Johnny was or when he would appear; though, she was certain he would and was prepared to give him some of the proceeds after she had sold up but was determined not to be pushed headlong into anything. On top of that, they did actually owe the bank money. Not a huge amount, they had been lucky, but it was still a debt that had to be settled.

All this was running through her head as she fed the working dogs and old Nellie, collected the eggs and did all her normal early morning jobs.

Having had a quick breakfast, she got in the ute and drove out to the furthest paddock where the young stock were. There was a creek running through here, which had always had a fair amount of water in it, the paddock itself also had the best feed, but it was a long way from the homestead and as such, Rachel had only managed to come and check them intermittently during the last few months. They were next on her list to sell and she had decided to get them back to the cattle yards in a few days to sort them out and put them in lots for transport.

As she got out to open the gate, she scanned the area but couldn't see any beasts nearby. She wasn't worried, though, as they had plenty of places to hide in away from the gate. However, as she bumped across the uneven ground towards the creek, she could still see no sign of them anywhere. Cresting the bank, which led down to the creek, she could see the mob standing around fascinated by something on the ground. Getting closer, Rachel could see to her growing horror a man's body laying half in and half out of the water. Even as she drew up and jumped out of the ute, she knew he was dead, but she still made herself check. He was lying face down. He was a big man and she had difficultly rolling him over. The cattle had poached the bank up around the body and everything was wet and muddy. Eventually she managed it and was relieved that it wasn't a face she recognised. He had a straggly grey beard and weather-beaten skin. His eyes were half-open, but Rachel couldn't tell what colour they were. His Akubra was trodden into the mud, his hair, which was a gingery colour, was quite long and he was very muddy all over.

Rachel's heart was racing, and she felt sick. She knew it would be no use trying to use her phone from here; there would be no signal. It meant going back to the house. But she felt bad about leaving him here with the cattle all round, and supposing someone or something had killed him, this area would be a crime scene. What to do she didn't really know but finally decided to drive the cattle off then high tail it home and ring for help.

The cattle by this time were losing interest and wandered off mostly without too much arm waving and shouting from Rachel. Once they had wandered off, she had another look at the strange man. She felt very sad for him and also very shaken by her discovery coming on top of last night's scare and confrontation with Johnny; it was all very upsetting.

More upsetting for the man's family than her though, she reasoned as she drove slowly back, how dreadful for them. How had he got there and where did he come from, who was he? These thoughts also crowded her mind.

She had a mobile, but the signal was shaky for much of the time, so she used the landline and called the police station.

'Rachel Conway here, is that Sergeant Parkins?'

'No, Mrs Conway, this is Josh Bulmer here, Sergeant Parkins has left, we have a new man here now, Sergeant Grimshaw, do you want to speak to him, or can I help you?'

Not wanting to speak to a new man, Rachel blurted out, 'I've just found a body, down by the creek. Can someone come?'

Tears were now threatening as the shock of her discovery took hold.

There was silence for a heartbeat then Josh said, 'We will be out there as soon as we can, don't touch anything. Are you okay? Not hurt or anything?'

'No, no, I'm fine, just come.'

'We'll be there as soon as we can, make yourself a cup of tea or something while you wait.'

Josh Bulmer knew Rachel as did most people in the small community, and everyone had a lot of time for her as they had for Sam, before he died.

Rachel put the phone down and settled in to wait.

CHAPTER 3

An hour and a half later, Josh drove up to the house in a cloud of dust. His police vehicle was closely followed by two others. One was a large black car. Rachel guessed that was for the body, and another with a man and a woman in it, they had an official look about them. Rachel met them at the bottom of the veranda steps.

'Hello, Mrs Conway, Rachel, sorry you have this to contend with, let me introduce you to our new sergeant.' Before he could say more, the sergeant, who had been standing behind Josh, stepped forward holding out his hand.

'I'm Mike Grimshaw, pleased to meet you though the circumstances could be better. Now where is this body you found?' This was all said quite quickly and Rachel hardly felt his hand, though he had offered to shake hands. He was already turning back to the police four-wheel drive and looking at Josh to go too.

Rachel ran to her ute saying 'follow me' while thinking *'boy is he in a hurry'* and before long, she got to the paddock gate where she had found the man. Stopping to open the gate, she stood to one side. Josh drew up as he got alongside her and she directed him to the creek, telling him where the body was. To her surprise, Sergeant Grimshaw got out of the car and said he would stay and talk to Rachel for a few minutes while the rest of them went on.

Rachel now had a chance to get a proper look at him. He was quite tall with thick light brown hair, his nose looked as if it had been broken at some point; he wasn't handsome, but he had warm brown eyes and just now they were regarding Rachel keenly.

'Are you alright? Josh told me you recently lost your husband and carrying on by yourself; it must be tough.'

His words caught her with such surprise that to her horror, Rachel found her eyes flood with tears; she turned her head away feeling very embarrassed, though, Mike had seen the tears.

'I...I'm fine,' she stuttered, 'just a bit shocked. I don't know how he got there or where he came from, he could hardly walk there.'

Mike continued to look at her a few moments longer. He saw a woman with dark blonde hair and grey eyes who at one time had been very attractive but now looked careworn and tired. She wore faded jeans with a rip near the knee, an old blue shirt and a very battered Akubra.

'Why don't you go back to the house now and leave this to us, we don't need you here just now.'

'But it is a bit of a walk to the creek from here,' Rachel protested.

'No worries it'll do me good, haven't had much exercise these last few days. Go on, off you go.'

'Okay, if you are sure.' Rachel got back in the ute thankfully and turned for home. Mike Grimshaw watched her go thoughtfully, then turned and securing the gate, set off across the paddock.

However, when Rachel reached home, she couldn't settle to anything, her mind was all over the place then a sudden horrible thought struck her; *was the man something to do with Johnny, no surely not, couldn't be, it just couldn't be.*

She paced the floor, longing for them to come back but dreading it; also, what to do if they asked any questions that might implicate Johnny. But then why would they, they couldn't know he had been there the night before and anyway she was letting her imagination run away with her.

She decided to clean, it was good therapy and before long, she was dusting, polishing and sweeping all at top speed. She picked up the old rug from the kitchen floor and on taking it outside, hung it up to give it a good thrashing to remove all the hair and dust it had accumulated.

She was so busy both with her thoughts and her basher; she didn't hear the police arrive back until there was a loud cough behind her, making her jump.

'God, you scared me,' she said crossly turning to face the two officers.

'Sorry, Mrs Conway,' Josh said. 'We didn't mean to scare you.'

'Rachel please, you've known me long enough, what happens now?'

'We need to ask you a few questions, Rachel,' said Sergeant Grimshaw. 'Perhaps we could go indoors?'

Rachel turned and led the way back inside. Everything was rather topsy-turvy where she had been cleaning, but she decided they'd have to put up with it. 'Tea, coffee?' she asked them as they settled themselves at the kitchen table.

'We have a few questions we need to ask you,' said the sergeant after they had both got a steaming coffee in front of them.

'First of all, are you sure you had never seen the deceased before?'

Rachel shook her head. 'Positive.'

'Just before the track becomes rough about six hundred metres from this house, we found what look like motorbike tracks and although we don't think the deceased was on a motorbike, can you explain them? You don't have a bike, Josh was telling me.'

Rachel sat with her head down, looking at her hands, which she had wrapped around her coffee cup. Many thoughts raced through her head, but in the end, she just said, 'I haven't a clue, I didn't notice them.'

Mike sat looking at her, he knew she was lying yet she didn't seem the type, why was she, what had she got to hide? They hadn't found anything that suggested foul play down at the creek; though, the cattle had poached the ground up so much it was a job to tell. They had found footprints on the edge of the creek the other side though, which looked as if they belonged to the deceased. They had set in motion a larger search of the area there, but it wasn't that far to Rachel's boundary fence so they would have to search the next-door place as well.

'We'll have to get in touch with your neighbour Sid Newberry and talk to him; I think we need to search over there.'

Rachel raised her head and looked at Mike when he said this; he saw the pain in her eyes. What was this all about?

'Okay, do you want me to ring him for you now?' Rachel was desperate to shift Mike's attention away from her. His eyes seemed to be looking straight into her soul. He un-nerved her.

Josh got to his feet. 'It's okay, Rachel, I'll speak to him, after all he is my father-in-law.'

Mike got to his feet too; there was plenty of time to talk to Rachel if necessary. He'd get to the bottom of her lying too in the end so for now he just said, 'Thank you, Rachel, we'll let ourselves out.' With that, he was gone.

CHAPTER 4

Rachel found it even harder to concentrate on anything after they had gone than before. She wandered about aimlessly, Nellie at her heels. Finally she went into Sam's tiny office, more of a cupboard really, had in fact been one before, and sat looking at the paperwork that was scattered about. Two days ago, she had been looking for the stud papers for one of the cows and had left it rather untidy. Somehow, it felt like a lifetime ago. Shaking her head at herself, she got to work to tidy it all up. Sorting papers was not distracting enough and her mind kept wandering. Then the telephone rang and made her jump. She realised that she had fallen asleep. Going to the telephone, which was in the passageway just outside the office, she picked up the receiver with a shaking hand. It was Mike Grimshaw.

'Rachel,' he said without preamble, 'this is to let you know we think the man found at the creek entered your property through Sid Newberry's place as we have found an old ute abandoned just near the boundary fence not far from the creek. Also, I would like to talk to you again tomorrow morning at nine thirty, is that convenient?'

Rachel was first relieved then worried again at his words, however she could hardly refuse as it would make matters worse.

'Y...Yes, of course. I... I am glad you found out a little more.' Rachel was kicking herself; she knew she sounded pathetic, but she couldn't seem to help it.

'See you in the morning,' Mike rang off before she had a chance to reply.

By now the sun was setting and Rachel realised she had existed almost solely on hot drinks all day, although she didn't feel hungry, she was too wound up. When finally she crawled into bed, she was too strung up to sleep. She lay listening for noises, any noises, and when old Nellie sneezed just outside on the veranda, she jumped out of her skin. Over the years, she had got used to Sam being away from home sometimes and wasn't by nature a nervous person but since he had died she had felt more alone especially at night. Now she admitted to herself that she was afraid. What of, she wasn't entirely sure, but what with Johnny's appearance then the dead body, she felt panicky and frightened. She had always left all the blinds open, they were so far from anyone it didn't matter, but tonight she had gone round the house drawing them. Some hadn't been moved for years and were difficult to shift, though others went well. As she lay there though, she found it claustrophobic and creeping out of bed in the dark, she drew them back carefully. It was a dark night; the moon was too young to brighten up the countryside; though, the stars were shining. It all looked so peaceful and quiet. Rachel chided herself for being a scaredy cat. She crept back into bed, but it was a long time before she got her heart rate down and then managed to get some sleep. Several times, she woke through the night and lay listening with her heart racing but could hear nothing.

Consequently, she overslept, and it was nearly seven before she scrambled out of bed. She had steeled herself to get up early and go to the back paddock and look through the young cattle as she had set out to do the previous morning. Looking worriedly at the clock she decided she wouldn't have time to do it properly and it was best left until Sergeant Grimshaw had been. Her appetite seemed to have returned in a small part as she had hardly eaten the day before so she made herself breakfast and got on with doing her normal jobs. As the time drew nearer, she became more and more apprehensive; she had guessed Grimshaw knew she was lying but what should she do? Should she tell him about Johnny? 'No way' she thought she didn't know if Johnny was mixed up in this or any other dubious activity, she didn't want to know. The thought then hit her and brought tears to her eyes that really she never wanted to see him again. She had experienced these feelings before, but now they were more intense. She was afraid of him, her own flesh and blood; it was a very sobering thought.

In the event Grimshaw was late and when he finally drew up in a cloud of dust, he looked as if he was living up to his name;he looked grim.

Rachel met him at the top of the veranda steps. 'Good Morning, Sergeant, would you like a drink?' Rachel had decided to be as charming as possible, maybe she could get away with it. Whatever 'it' was.

'Morning, Rachel, I'll have a drink in a minute, thanks.'

Rachel indicated the chairs nearby and the policeman sat down and Rachel followed suit.

He gave her a penetrating look. 'I know I have only just met you, but I can tell when someone is lying. Particularly when they aren't used to lying and are not very good at it. Why did you lie to me, Rachel, about the motorbike tyre tracks?'

Rachel sat staring at him. She didn't know what to say, but she knew she would have to come clean.

The tears that seemed more prevalent since Sam died resurfaced and gulping she said in a low voice, 'My son was here the other night. I don't think he had anything to do with the man you found but, but...'

Mike thrust a clean handkerchief into her hands and let her cry for a minute until she had control of herself.

'I've heard about your son, Johnny, is it?' Rachel nodded. 'Small town gossip right?' Again, Rachel nodded unable to speak; her throat was too closed up.

'What time was he here?'

'About 1.40 am, I think.'

'What time did he leave?'

'I'm not sure, about 2.30 maybe. It might have been a bit later I'm not sure,' Rachel was nearly shredding the hankie as she said this.

Mike put his hand on top of hers and stopped her, 'Leave me something to blow my nose on.'

'Gosh, I'm sorry.'

'We don't know why the man died yet nor who he was, though that should be resolved this morning so long as the ute wasn't stolen or anything, so no jumping to conclusions, okay?'

Rachel nodded.

'Why don't we have a coffee now and save my poor hankie, what do you reckon?'

Rachel just nodded unable to speak again, she always had found it harder to cope when people were kind, ever since Sam had died, and she could keep her cool so long as friends and neighbours were practical, but as soon as they said kind words, she would collapse into tears. She hated that,, but it was how she was and she couldn't seem to control it. Getting to his feet, Mike gently took the now sodden hankie from her and pulled her to her feet. Then he went with her into the house, almost guiding her gently, with his hand lightly on her back.

Rachel busied herself making coffee and by the time she sat down across the table from Mike, she was quite composed.

'Tell me about Johnny. I've heard the gossip, now I'd like to hear the truth.'

Drawing a deep breath, Rachel told Mike all she felt able to say about Johnny. What a sweet boy he had been, the accident; right up until the present. Once she had started, she found it easier than she expected and before long, she was telling Mike about Sam, his illness and how it had taken them both by surprise. He was a good listener and just sat watching her and not interrupting at all, just nodding occasionally.

Finally, she stopped. 'Oh God, whatever must you think of me going on and on like that. I don't know what came over me, I'm so sorry.'

Mike smiled, it lit his whole rather austere face up and he looked almost handsome. 'Nah, don't be, I asked and it's good to let these things out. I am guessing it's rather lonely out here, so you don't get much chance to unload. Also, it helps me understand things. I'm new to the district, not just the town, so I am in the dark about a lot of things.

'Is it alright if I go back to the paddock now? I need to have a good look at the youngsters down there.'

Mike stood up and glanced at his watch. 'Let me touch base then I will come with you,' he said.

Rachel looked at him in surprise, she hadn't expected that, but she was dreading going back there. Feeling grateful she just said, 'If you've time, I expect you need to have another look?'

'Something like that, yep.' Mike went to talk into his radio.

CHAPTER 5

As they drove out towards the paddock, Mike constantly asked questions about the farm; how many bores were there, how many cattle had they run in the past, what bloodlines were they. As soon as she had answered one question, he asked another. So Rachel painstakingly explained that she had just over a hundred cows and two bulls all pedigree Brahmans; that they had built the breeding herd up themselves as Sam's father wasn't interested in stud cattle, he just bred for meat. By the time they got to the gate into the back paddock, Rachel felt quite worn out, so as Mike was about to get out and open the gate she said, 'Why all those questions? They haven't any bearing on the dead man, you're the first policeman I've come across who wants to know about cattle blood lines.'

Again, he flashed his rare smile at her. 'Sorry, I got a bit carried away there. I am the youngest son of a cattle breeder out west. My three brothers are working with Dad on the property, but there wasn't enough for me too, so here I am. I would love to have a place of my own one day; though, it's probably just a dream.'

'Oh, I see, so you are a country boy at heart then?' It was Rachel's turn to smile now.

As they drove into the paddock, they could see the cattle some way off and to Rachel's relief nowhere near the creek. They drove nearer, then Rachel got out to have a better inspection. Mike got out too and watched her closely as she walked around looking at them.

Rachel didn't say anything and nor did Mike until a short time later when they were on their way back. 'Well, what do you reckon?' Mike asked eventually.

Rachel glanced at him. 'Sorry, I was miles away. I will get them up and sell all but a few, the younger ones need more meat on them I think if they are to go to the meat works.'

Mike was silent again then he said, 'I don't need to be told to mind my own business, but I will say this anyway. Are you sure you are right to sell some of those young heifers for meat? They are fine beasts; the other thing is, how are you going to get them back on your own?'

'I'll ask Sid Newberry to give me a hand; he has been these last few months. As for selling the best, I don't know what else I can do. I can't manage out here on my own for too long, I have to sell.'

Mike looked very thoughtful, then said, 'I can see your dilemma. I guess you have to do what you have to do. It's a shame, though. You have some lovely heifers there. Why not just sell off a few that aren't so good and see how it goes?'

Rachel felt rather resentful. He was in a way repeating what she had just said but changing it round to keeping most and just selling a few and anyway it was none of his business.

'I'll see,' she said shortly.

Mike glanced at her; he had overstepped the mark he knew, after all, he hardly knew the woman.

When they got back to the homestead, Mike thanked her for allowing him to see her cattle and without waiting for a reply got in his car and drove off, not wanting to put his foot in it any further.

Rachel watched him go with mixed feelings. It wasn't his business but what he said had been right. Just how badly did she need the money? But then the loneliness was getting to her, even more so since Johnny's visit. It was strange being afraid of her only son, but in truth, she was very afraid of him. There was a kind of latent menace in him that seemed to lurk there under the surface. Apart from old Nellie, she was so alone. Sid and his family lived a good ten kilometres by road, six across country, via the creek. It had never bothered her before; she had Sam and they had a couple of full-time men working for them. Then when their finances weren't so good they had employed casual staff as and when they were needed. Until Sam had become ill it hadn't mattered. They were both fit and healthy and thought they could go on forever. It hadn't worked like that, Rachel thought sadly, as she went about her chores. 'No,' she decided. '*I need to sell up and move into town, I will feel much better.*'

Later though after she had eaten a scratch supper, she got up to draw the blinds again as she had the night before, then looking out, she could see everything bathed in the moonlight, which would soon be gone. It looked so magical and peaceful. It was all hers, everywhere she looked in this huge open space it was hers. She felt she knew every grain of earth, every tree, every plant, the wild animals big and small, how she would feel living back amongst people again?

With a sigh, she drew the blinds and cleared up her supper. Going into the little office, she sat down to go through her finances yet again. Mike had made her doubt her resolve to sell and she wanted to make sure that in a practical sense it was the right thing to do.

Again, in the night, she awoke with a start, but the sound that had disturbed her was rain hammering on the roof. It made her smile to herself, as rain was always welcome in this part of the country. When she looked out the next morning it looked as if a giant had emptied a huge bag of gemstones across the paddocks and her garden. The whole place was sparkling with drops of rain and the fresh smell of wet earth made her feel again that this was her place to be.

CHAPTER 6

Two days later, Sid arrived with a horse float and two of his men to help Rachel drive the cattle back to the yards near the homestead. Rachel still had her own horse who, though getting on in years, was good enough for what she needed him to do. She was rather surprised however, when Sid unloaded four horses. They were all saddled up ready to go.

'Hello, Sid, what's with the extra horse, old Spot here is still up for today's work?'

'Hi, Rach, it's not for you, it's for that new copper, said he wanted to come along, seems he knows about cattle and also said you wouldn't mind. Think he's got the day off or something.' Sid shrugged his shoulders.

Just then, Mike arrived looking ready to roll wearing boots, jeans, an old shirt and Akubra at a jaunty angle on his head.

'Hello, folks, are you all waiting for me? Sorry, took longer than I thought to get away. I have some news on that poor bastard you found in the creek, Rachel. He died of natural causes it seems, his liver was pretty much trashed, and his heart was dodgy too.'

'Oh.' Rachel was at a loss on what to say. She was feeling cross about Mike coming along without her knowing beforehand, but now she was feeling relieved that there wasn't a sinister cause to the man's death. 'Where did he come from, though?'

Alan, one of Sid's men who had come along, spoke up now, 'As I told the sergeant, this bloke turned up looking for work, the boss was in town so I told him to bugger off; he reeked of booze. He must have driven across towards your place and well, you know the rest. He was pretty drunk when I saw him.'

'The ute had quite a few empty whisky bottles rolling around both in the cab and the tray. Our guess is he got as far as the fence and decided to walk.

Didn't know what he was doing. If the creek hadn't been low, he wouldn't have made it across. We found his footmarks on the other bank.'

'Do you know who he was or where he came from?' asked Rachel.

'No, the ute was unregistered and pretty old. He had no identification, but we think he came from WA. As that is what the old plate on the ute said, mind you, that might not be right. I expect we will find out in the end. We are looking at the missing persons files just now.'

Rachel found it all rather sad and was silent as they rode out to the back paddock. It took the next two and a half hours to get the cattle back and into the yards. Fortunately, they were very co-operative and had been near the gate too, which meant they didn't have to ride around the paddock rounding them up. Rachel's dogs were efficient too, and it all helped to make it a smooth operation.

Once they were yarded Sid loaded his horses, and after his men and himself had a quick smoko, they left. Sid promised he would come back the next day and help sort the young cattle out.

Mike looked at Rachel as she was clearing up the empty mugs and tipping the crumbs on the veranda for old Nellie. He could see she wasn't very relaxed despite the easy morning the cattle had given them all.

'What is it, Rachel, have I upset you or is it something else?'

Rachel put down the things she was about to carry inside.

'Well, it would have been nice if you had said to me you intended to come this morning; though, I suppose that is silly as Sid could have said and you were a help. Also, I think it's all rather sad about that man. How old do you think he was?'

'Early sixties we are guessing. He had a rough life by the looks of it, a broken leg at some time in his life, quite a few old scars. I would say he might even have been a bronco rider or some such, a drover, who knows. There was a filthy old swag, a billy and the remains of food in an esky that had seen better days in the ute.'

Rachel nodded; occasionally, they had itinerant men turn up wanting a few days' work. They had always helped them if they could; they had always been called swagmen, but it didn't seem to fit these days so well as they didn't travel on foot anymore, though in every other way the name fitted.

Rachel looked at her watch. 'I haven't much to offer you, but do you want a bite of lunch before you got back to town, a kind of thank you?'

Mike hesitated, 'If you are sure, I didn't mean to muscle in and annoy you this morning. I just had a yen to be back on a horse, driving cattle.'

Rachel smiled at him. The first that day. 'It's okay, I understand, all I can offer is scrambled eggs. Cupboard's a bit bare, I haven't stocked up for ages.'

'I'll do it, just show me where the things are, you look tired, take a seat and let me loose in your kitchen. I have the day off so I have plenty of time.'

Rather surprised at herself, Rachel let him. As she sat watching, she suddenly asked, 'Are you married Mike?' He seemed so sufficient cooking that he seemed like a man who was used to looking after himself.

'Was, still am technically. I have two children; they are both with their mother in Brisbane.'

'How old are they?' Rachel saw his shoulders tense up as he spoke but wanted to know and now seemed a good time.

'Ben is six and Em is nearly eight. Now get stuck into Grimshaw's special scrambled eggs.' With that, he placed a steaming plate of golden fluffy eggs in front of her. Rachel's mouth watered, she hadn't been eating well since Sam died, couldn't be bothered much of the time, there seemed no point, but these eggs looked so good she actually felt hungry.

Mike hid his amusement at how quickly she devoured the eggs but refrained from saying anything. She was so thin he thought she wasn't eating properly, but he didn't want to draw attention to the fact he had noticed.

After they had eaten, Rachel made more tea and they discussed cattle a while longer, then Mike took his leave, thanking her for the day though Rachel thought it was the other way around.

In bed that night, Rachel thought about the day's events and admitted to herself that Mike had been a great help.

CHAPTER 7

The next morning, Sid rang to say he had so much on and would Rachel mind if he put off coming to help for a couple of days. Rachel was disappointed but needed his help so said it was fine. She walked around the yard making mental notes about the heifers. She sighed, she didn't like the thought of sending them away for meat but then nor did she relish the prospect of getting buyers in to sell them as breeders, she felt damned if she did and damned if she didn't. Her thoughts turned to Mike and his assertion that in the long run it would be better to keep them for the time being at least. As for the property itself, she would have to wait for probate, though she was okay selling cattle as they had a partnership agreement. The farm was Sam's, he had inherited it from his father, and it had been in the family for generations. Sam's mother was still going strong and she lived on the Gold Coast where Sam's two sisters both lived. A million miles away from the farm. Sam's father had died in a car accident when Sam was twenty not long before he met Rachel.

Rachel went back to the house to look once again at the papers and documents she had for the cattle.

While she was indoors the phone rang, it was Mike. He came straight to the point after saying hello. Would she mind very much if he came out when Sid came back as he was interested to see them sorting the heifers.

'No, I suppose not.' Rachel felt doubtful though why, she couldn't say.

Mike heard the doubt in her voice and said, 'Look, Rachel, if it's a problem I'll stay away.'

After she had put the phone down, Rachel sat frowning. Why was he so interested in her cattle, was she missing something? Maybe he was just lonely and enjoyed being out on the farm. He certainly had baggage; she was surprised his children weren't older as she thought he was in his early to mid-forties. She realised with a jolt she found him attractive, not his looks, but his warm personality. He seemed a very caring person, like Sam.

Giving herself a shake, she put all thoughts of Mike and the heifers behind her and letting the dogs loose, got in the ute with her tools and set off to make sure the boundary fence was all good. It would take her the two days until Sid came back to do this. She had been meaning to for a couple of months now, but other things had got in the way. She loved being out in the paddocks, the big blue sky, the gum trees with their unique smell, the small hills and the silvery creeks that ran through the little valleys, although coming as they were into spring the creeks were dry. The winter has been exceptionally dry, though. Rachel thought they were lucky as she still had enough feed left. Sam had always been careful not to overstock, and in seasons like this, it paid off. Rachel sighed; she missed him so much. He had a lovely dry sense of humour and was so warm-hearted and generous, his blue eyes would twinkle as he teased her about something she had done or said. The only blot on their lives had been Johnny. '*Johnny! He said he'd be back, not yet, not ever I hope,*' thought Rachel to herself. Sam hadn't said much before he died, but Rachel knew that his son had broken his heart. He had always tried to hide it, but Rachel knew it was there eating away at him. So long as they didn't talk about it or him, they were fine, but sometimes it would surface and Sam's eyes would be full of pain. Sam had made just the small provision in his will for Johnny, saying it would be up to Rachel to make it more later if she wanted to.

Rachel stopped, there was a sag in the wire just by some old tree stumps, so she got out with her strainers to pull the wire tight. As she walked round the end of the largest stump; a big brown snake that had been coiled there reared up at her. She leapt back and catching her heel on a rock tumbled over backwards. Jet, one of the three dogs that were in the tray of the ute, jumped out and started to bark madly at the snake, which Rachel had thought was about to strike. The snake changed its mind and slithered away under the fence.

Rachel was winded and sore, she sat up gingerly, her wrist really hurt. Jet thought it was great fun having Rachel on the ground and seconds later, the other two dogs jumped down and joined in. It took a lot of scolding on Rachel's part to get them to leave her alone so she could get up. She looked at her wrist, it was swelling and at an odd angle, she was feeling very nauseous and the pain was intense. She propped herself on the tree stump and tried to breathe deeply; she felt so sick, what should she do?

After a time, the dizziness subsided and telling the dogs to get back up onto the tray, she hauled herself into the driver's seat. No sooner had she sat down then she realised she had left her tools on the ground by the fence. By this time, she was bathed in sweat as every time she moved the pain shot up her arm. She tried to hold her arm against her body in such a way to protect it, but nothing seemed to help. Her tools would have to stay there, she decided. She had to twist her body at an odd angle to reach the ignition key and start the vehicle, then she could put it in gear and drive home. Not that easy as the ground was very bumpy, she used her knees too, which helped with the steering a little. Then she got to the gate into the next paddock which she had shut, as there were cows in this paddock. She heard herself groaning as she clambered out clumsily. It seemed to take a lifetime to get back in this fashion. Never had opening and shutting gates been so difficult, never had she felt so alone, if only there was someone to help, but of course there was no one, just the wide-open spaces, her dogs and herself.

Finally, she drew up near the house. She hadn't the energy to tie the dogs up; she hoped they wouldn't go far. She fumbled opening the door and went straight into the bathroom. Getting her boots off wasn't too bad. It took longer to get her jeans off, but how was she going to get her shirt off she didn't know. It took a very long time just to undo the buttons with one hand and easing it down, her broken wrist nearly had her fainting. She slid her bra straps off her shoulders and managed to slide it all the way down. She had lost enough weight lately that it was quite easy. The warm water made her feel better as her back was very sore. She had actually landed on a large flat rock when she fell, her coccyx hurt too, but the water restored her a little.

However, all the good was undone when the water became tepid and she stepped out of the shower. Drying herself proved very awkward. In the end she gave up and finding an old dressing gown of Sam's, wrapped herself up as best she could. She went to the first aid box so she could bind her wrist up; however, undoing it proved impossible as the catch was stuck fast, and she couldn't do it with one hand. Then she realised that her fingers on her right hand were numb. 'Oh God,' she said aloud, knowing it meant that the nerves were compromised. Shaking with pain, shock and worry, she went to the telephone and rang Sid being her nearest neighbour, no reply. Norma, his wife, normally answered the phone, but it seemed no one was in the house. Mobile reception was very sketchy out here and Rachel only could use hers when she was nearer town.

In the end, she rang Jane, her closet friend in town. Jane ran the local bakery and Rachel hoped she wouldn't be so busy now as it was long past lunchtime.

'Hi, Rach, how are you?' Jane's cheery voice came over the phone and the sound made Rachel choke back the tears.

'Not so good, Jane, I've broken my arm, well my wrist I think. I... I need some help.'

Rachel had never asked for help with anything before and it was difficult, but she knew she must.

'Oh God, you poor thing, hang in there. I'll organise the troops, someone will be with you shortly, can you manage until then? Will you be okay?'

'Yes, yes, I'll be fine, thanks, Jane.'

'Okay,' Jane rang off, wanting to get organised to help. Rachel lay on the sofa in the corner of the big old kitchen still huddled in Sam's old dressing gown. She would worry about finding some clothes later as it would be sometime before anyone got there.

CHAPTER 8

Rachel woke with a start; someone was standing beside her. For a moment, she couldn't think where she was and why she was asleep on the sofa in Sam's old dressing gown. The pain kicked in as she moved and the whole sorry mess came rushing back. She squinted up at the person who was speaking, still not fully awake. It was Dr Bradley and he was telling her it was lucky he was already out this way, so it was easy for him to come to her. One of the men on Sid's place had come off a young horse he was breaking and got concussion, so Merv, as everybody called him, had been called out.

'Seems to be a day for accidents, now let's look at this wrist.'

Merv shook his head and tutted when he saw Rachel's wrist and arm. 'If Jane had called me ten minutes earlier you could have gone with the flying doctor straight into hospital. Young Stan has a head injury, so I got them to come and take him. You can't be too careful with heads. Now, my dear, you will have to come with me I'm afraid, this needs an operation. I'm thinking, else you might lose the use of at least part of your hand; there is pressure on the nerves. You will have to have an x-ray, but just looking I can see it's broken, and your hand is going blue, circulation is compromised it seems.'

Merv helped her to her feet. 'I need to put some clothes on,' muttered Rachel. She was extremely embarrassed when the doctor followed her to the bedroom, as it was a tip. However, he helped her find some loose trousers and a loose shirt and averted his eyes as much as he could while helping her dress. Rachel reminded herself that he had seen quite a few of her personal places over the years anyway, though this was slightly different. She dispensed with wearing a bra; it would be too difficult. She just shook her head when Merv asked her.

She felt very untidy and uncomfortable when finally, she said she was ready to go. Merv had phoned Sid and spoken to Norma who said one of them would see to the dogs and take old Nellie back with them, as Rachel didn't want to leave the old dog on her own. As she went down the veranda steps, a wave of giddiness swept over Rachel and she almost fell. Merv grabbed her and before she could protest, picked her up and set her in the passenger seat of his big four by four. He was a short, stocky man who was well known for his strength; with his thick glasses and baldhead, people who didn't know him often underestimated both his intellect and his strength. No one knew how old he was; he seemed timeless and had been the local doctor ever since Rachel had been out at the farm.

The movement of the last little while had set the pain up again. Merv had looked at her back but thought it was just severe bruising. Just now though she hurt all over. 'Do you want some pain killers, or are you good to go?' Merv asked her.

Gritting her teeth Rachel said, 'Just go, I want this over with.'

Merv gave a grim smile. 'Well, hang on I'll go as slowly as I can, but it will still be a rough ride till we get to the bitumen.'

Every little jolt seemed to send white-hot fire through her arm and down her back, and although not far, it seemed to take forever to get to the smoother surface.

Eventually, they got to the little town and Merv stopped to call in at his surgery then they started the rather longer drive to Roma. Merv thought Rachel needed surgery and if she was lucky, the flying surgeon may be there to see her.

However, she would have to wait a couple of days, they found when they got there. Merv disappeared while the paperwork was being done but reappeared soon with a toothbrush, hairbrush and a nightdress. This highly embarrassed Rachel, but Merv waved his hand. 'All in a day's work, but I am afraid I will have to be getting back now, you are in good hands. I'll let Jane know where you are.' And with a wave of his hand he was gone.

Rachel felt the tears pricking her eyes as she was helped into bed by a kindly nurse. She felt so alone more than ever, which was silly as she was being looked after so well and there were all these people around her.

Rachel couldn't sleep that night, to her it was noisy and there was muted light coming from outside her room. She was thankful she had a room to herself, but it was all too strange and upsetting. Also, it brought back memories of the time Sam had been in hospital, though he had died at home.

She moved and wriggled as much as she could to get comfortable. She didn't want to think about Sam just now. It was silly she reflected that she hadn't slept well at home especially since Johnny's visit; partly because she was so nervous at night, now there was no need to be and she still couldn't sleep.

The next day dragged by. They x-rayed her wrist and bound it up, but she would have to wait to see the surgeon. Jane rang and so did Norma, but both conversations were brief as Rachel hadn't got her mobile with her, so they had rung through on the hospital phone. For this reason, they didn't talk for long. Her wrist and arm throbbed, and she felt teary and bored. She was allowed to go to the sitting area but no further but she wasn't much of a one for watching television.

The next morning, she was first on the list, so everything happened early for her. They told her she could go home later that day and they had spoken to Dr Bradley and he said he would organise it. Afterwards, Rachel couldn't remember the name of the surgeon, although he spoke to her before and after the operation. She would be referred to the small cottage hospital nearer home for any further assessment or treatment if necessary.

It was all over quickly for Rachel. One minute she was waiting to feel sleepy, the next minute she was being shaken awake.

Two thirty, she was sitting in her rather raggy clothes waiting yet again for someone to collect her and hoping against hope it would be Jane.

Then to her consternation, who should walk in but Mike. He was dressed in uniform and Rachel was so taken aback that her greeting was, 'What are you doing here?'

'Hi, Rachel, well, giving you a lift home, at least that was the plan.'

'But don't you have work to do, traffic, burglary, something useful, not me.' Rachel knew she was talking nonsense but couldn't seem to stop herself.

'Well, since you asked, I did have to come to town on police business, but I'm clear now so are you good to go?'

Rachel was even more aware of her dishevelled appearance than before and got to her feet reluctantly. She didn't understand why exactly, but she was very conscious that she wasn't wearing a bra and hoped Mike wouldn't notice.

Mike, however, seemed very laid back about everything, as if it was normal to pick up women from the hospital that he hardly knew and deliver them home.

He didn't take her home but straight to Jane's place as they had talked about it and decided that Rachel would want a few days to get used to only being able to use one hand. It was the best part of a couple of hours back, but Mike and Rachel fell into an easy conversation and in spite of her initial reserve, Rachel enjoyed the drive back. Mike made her feel relaxed, and before long, her eyes closed, and she fell asleep. She awoke with a start. 'Not long now, be back soon.' Mike grinned across at her.

'Oh God, I'm sorry I didn't mean to fall asleep.' Rachel felt embarrassed all over again.

'Look, Rachel, I realise you don't really know me, but please let me help you over the next few weeks because you will need help especially with the arm of yours. I can only help when not on duty, obviously, but it would be something I would love to do. Getting on a horse again, driving cattle, all that stuff. I miss it more than I knew I did and coming out to your place has given me a big boost mentally, so please don't refuse. You'll be doing me a favour, not the other way round.' Mike sounded serious, and Rachel thought she detected a longing in his voice. She sat quietly for a few minutes, weighing the pros and cons in her head.

Finally, she said, 'There will be gossip; you know what small towns are like.'

Mike grinned across at her briefly. 'That sounds as if you might agree.'

'Well, what you have said makes sense. I will need help so we will just have to make it plain, if anyone says anything, that it is strictly a business arrangement. However, that said; I can't really afford to pay you.'

Mike shrugged. 'I hadn't given payment a thought, just being out at your place will be payment enough.'

Soon after that, they arrived at Jane's. Jane and her husband lived just down the road from the bakery and Rachel and she had been friends ever since Rachel had come into the district and had then become Sam's wife.

CHAPTER 9

Jane bustled around Rachel so much that in the end Rachel said, 'Jane, please don't try so hard, I've only broken my arm, it's no big deal just uncomfortable and inconvenient.'

Bob, Jane's husband came in just then; he worked in the local hardware store. 'Hi, Rachel, Jane said you were here to stay for a couple of days or so, how's the arm? Have you been given the full Jane treatment yet?'

Jane flicked the tea towel she had in her hand at him, 'Watch it you, I'm just trying to make sure Rachel has everything she needs and is comfortable.'

'Honestly, Jane, there is no need to fuss, you are so kind, I...' Rachel stopped and swallowed the threatening tears, she was being pathetic she knew but ever since Johnny's visit and then finding the body she had felt stressed and teary.

Jane understood, Rachel had a tough year behind her, and it seemed as if it was still a tough one. She patted Rachel's shoulder and then called her family that dinner was ready. She had two girls, Beth and Angie, who though in their late teens still lived at home and a son, Clive, who had long since left home but ironically had come home for a quick visit. Rachel had felt bad when she learnt this but was assured the sleeping arrangements were fine and not to worry.

It was good to be with the family. Rachel missed Sam, she did, and mostly in recent years there had been just the two of them; though, on occasions like Christmas there would be family get-togethers, though last Christmas Sam had been so ill and had died on Boxing Day. Sam's family had been there, and Rachel's father and brother. Rachel's parents were divorced, and her mother lived down in Victoria. They weren't close and Rachel hadn't seen her for some years, just the odd phone call now and again. So, it was a balm to Rachel's spirit to be with people she knew so well and was comfortable with. Although, she slept on a pull-out bed in the girl's room. Rachel slept deeply and peacefully.

The next morning, Jane asked her how she had slept, and Rachel told her it was the best sleep she'd had since Sam died.

The next four days flew by for Rachel; she was pampered more than she wanted to be but got the hang of using her other hand more and found if she was careful, she could still use the fingers on her broken side a little, though she had to be careful. Jane lent her some clothes but not a bra as Rachel was rather better endowed than Jane, but as she stayed close to the house, she wasn't worried. In fact, she rather enjoyed the freedom.

Bob said he would drive her home and Sid had been in touch to say that Norma had been over and cleaned the house and tidied up. Sid had also sent one of his men around the boundary fence to make sure it was all in order, and they had retrieved Rachel's tools.

By the time Rachel got home, she was pleased to be back, rather to her surprise, as she had felt so unsettled out there of late. Maybe a break was what she had needed, she thought to herself though not one like that.

Soon after Bob had gone, she found some of her more usual clothes to wear; she managed a bra by doing it up at the front and pulling it round; she felt more like her old self. A short time later, Sid and Norma turned up and Norma bustled about making sure everything was as easy for Rachel as possible. She had made a huge casserole and divided it up into smaller helpings, telling Rachel to freeze them. Both women laughed then, as Norma said, 'Listen to me, grandmother and sucking eggs comes to mind.'

When Sid and Norma finally left, though, Rachel felt the loneliness return stronger than ever. She told herself she was being silly as when Sam was away with the cattle or just across the property, she had never worried. This was very different though, and Johnny's visit had rattled her more than she had thought possible.

She found that it wasn't so easy to work her rather ancient shower either and the shower at Jane's had easy turn taps, not old stiff ones like hers. It took a long time to shower and get ready for bed. She went through the routine of drawing all the curtains and blinds, even though she had told herself she wouldn't do it when she had been staying at Jane's.

Nellie seemed restless too, which added to Rachel's unease. She was just getting into bed when the phone rang. She sat on the edge of the bed, her heart racing. Should she answer it? It wouldn't be Jane as they had spoken not long before, or Norma, was it Johnny?

She got up and with shaking hands answered it. 'H...Hello?'

'Hi, Rachel, sorry to ring late, how are you?' Mike said.

Relief flooded through Rachel. 'OH! Mike, oh yes, I'm fine, thanks.'

Mike had picked up her hesitation or was it fear? 'Are you sure? You sound a bit worried'

'Absolutely, thanks, Mike.' Rachel forced herself to sound light-hearted.

'Alright if I come out tomorrow?'

'Yes, it would be good as Sid said he will come out with some of his men and finally sort those cattle.'

'See you tomorrow then, night.' And he was gone. Rachel thought she should be getting used to his brevity on the phone by now.

CHAPTER 10

Struggling to get dressed the next morning, Rachel reflected on her conversation with Mike the night before. He was always very brief on the phone, but she was getting used to that although it always seemed to surprise her. She hadn't slept at all well, waking up thinking she could hear noises, more cat napping than sleeping, but she was actually looking forward to the day as, though she couldn't do much herself, there would be company and hustle and bustle, it would be good she thought.

She was just finishing her bowl of cereal when she heard a car and going to the door, she was in time to see Mike climb out of his ute. He seemed to hesitate and look around before turning to the house.

'Mike,' she called.

He was looking serious as he came towards her but then grinned. 'How're you doing?'

'Good thanks, have a cuppa before we make a start?' She felt ridiculously pleased to see him.

'Yeah, why not, a coffee would go down well, thanks,' he said as he mounted the veranda steps.

Rachel found herself chattering away nineteen to the dozen about all sorts of things, maybe it was because she was suddenly aware of his presence or nerves or what it was, she couldn't say. She just couldn't seem to stop chattering away about Jane and her family and how kind people were. At last, she ran out of steam.

Mike sat with his coffee in front of him looking at her with an amused expression on his face. 'You sound very upbeat this morning.'

'Yes well, at last I feel as if I'm getting somewhere if I can at least sort this cattle thing out. I feel as if everything has conspired against me this last week or so.'

Mike looked at her keenly. 'I know you want to sell, but are you really sure you are doing the right thing? I can imagine it can be a bit lonely out here, but this is your home. I can't see you living in town. How old were you when you first came here?'

'Twenty-one, Sam and I had a whirlwind romance I suppose you'd call it. Sam's dad had died shortly before we met. I came out as a student thinking I wanted to be a teacher, so I was sent here to do a stint at the school in town. I never made it away again.'

Just then, the dogs barked and looking out they saw Sid had arrived.

For the next couple of hours, it was dust, shouted orders and organised mayhem. At the end of it, Rachel wasn't at all sure if she had made the right choices. She had one small yard full and the big yard with still quite a few young heifers in it.

'Well, Rachel, are you going to sell these or not?' Sid had a lot to do on his own place and was slightly frustrated that Rachel seemed so unsure of what she actually wanted.

'Yes, though maybe not all of them,' Rachel indicated the larger group in the small yard, 'there are a few in there that maybe I should keep for now.'

Sid looked at her despairingly. 'You want to go through them again? Strewth woman, we'll be here all day!'

'Oh God, Sid, I'm sorry I'm not really sure what I'm doing. I wish Sam was here.' To her horror, her eyes filled with tears.

Sid immediately felt bad and put his arm around Rachel's shoulders. 'No worries, love, we can go through this mob and have another look at them. Alright, you lot, get cracking, you heard what the boss said.' Sid turned to the men who had been standing by. Mike too had been watching and listening to the exchange between Rachel and Sid.

An hour later, a much-reduced mob of cattle was earmarked for sale, while the others were to be let out into the home paddock.

Then back to the house for a very quick smoko before Sid and his men took off back home and more work.

'I had better ring the sale yards and get transport organised now,' Rachel said as she picked up the mugs one handed. She had hated standing by watching the activity this morning unable to actually do much, but at least some phone calls were something she could do.

Mike who had stayed behind nodded. 'I think you've done the right thing. There are some excellent beasts among those you've kept; it would be a shame to sell those for meat.'

Rachel gave him a brief smile. 'Thanks for your help today, have you got time for a bite of lunch?'

'Sure have, I've got the whole day as it happens, so any jobs that want doing I'm your man.'

Rachel did find him some jobs to do and, in the end, Mike didn't leave until it was just getting dark. Rachel felt guilty about that, but Mike brushed her concerns away and drove off with a cheery wave.

Before he went, he told her that they now had a name for the man found in the creek and that he had originally come from WA. He had travelled around picking up odd jobs here and there in later years, but the grog problem got bigger and bigger until he was hardly ever sober. He had been picked up by the police many times for minor offences but had never been in this part of Queensland before, so the local police hadn't anything on him.

CHAPTER 11

Rachel felt the atmosphere change when Mike had gone. Was it her imagination? Maybe, she told herself, but she couldn't help feeling even more alone than ever. She was really coping quite well with one hand she told herself as, if she was careful, she could kind of use the fingers on the broken side, as the break it turned out was half way up her arm, she supposed that helped. She had heated up part of the casserole Norma had made for lunch as Mike was there, so now she just wanted something easy and decided to get out a helping of soup she had put in the freezer some weeks ago.

The freezer and laundry were under the house so she fed Nellie then putting on the light from the kitchen, which she could do, she went to go and retrieve the soup. For some reason she couldn't explain, she felt quite spooked as she made her way down the steps and under the house. She looked around in the dim light, but everything seemed to be in the right place. Hurrying, she opened the freezer to get the soup, which was near the top in a basket, but it wasn't there!

Thinking she must have made a mistake, she rummaged as much as she could, but there was no soup anywhere. The hairs stood up on the back of her neck, the soup had gone. Johnny? She looked around, then down and saw three cigarette butts on the floor, she knew then she was right.

Had he had it when he had paid a visit the other night or had he snuck back since, maybe when she was away. Either way she wasn't at all happy, the fear returned and slamming the freezer door shut, she made her way shakily back to the kitchen. She sat down at the table and tried to reason with herself, he was her son after all, why was she frightened of him? He wouldn't hurt her, would he? She sat a long time with those thoughts racing around in her head, all hunger gone. Eventually, she got to her feet and put the kettle on to boil; she'd have a cup of tea then go to bed.

Later lying in bed, she chided herself for being a wimp; she really had to assert herself and stop being indecisive and be positive. Clinging onto these thoughts, she drifted off to sleep.

She woke with a jolt and like before, her heart was racing, her breathing ragged. She had heard something, what? Then she heard it again, the throaty roar of a motorbike in the distance, no not one, more than one. The dogs sat up barking just then, as the sound came closer; Rachel sat up in bed. She had made doubly sure all the doors were locked and since Johnny had been last time, she had let old Nellie sleep in the room beside the bed. She didn't know if she should put the light on or leave it off hoping they would think she was away and go away themselves, as by now, she was sure there were at least two bikes.

The sound of engines died then she heard the veranda steps creak and the door rattled. Then the footsteps came around the house and stopped outside her bedroom. By now, she was trembling all over and Nellie who had picked up on her fear was growling deep in her throat. 'MA, I know you are in there, let me and my mate in, I WANT TO TALK.'

'GO AWAY, JOHNNY, I have nothing to say to you.'

'JESUS, WOMAN,' Johnny yelled. 'OPEN THE BLOODY DOOR OR I'LL BREAK IT DOWN, YOU HEAR ME?'

'Alright, alright, give me a few minutes.'

'I'll give you two then I start bashing the door.' With that the footsteps went on to the back door.

Still shaking like a leaf, Rachel climbed out of bed and with difficultly, partly because of her arm and partly out of fear, got into her old dressing gown. Nellie by her side, she made it into the kitchen just as there was an almighty crash on the door. She threw it open just as Johnny was about to have another go at breaking it down, he nearly fell on top of her.

For a moment, mother and son were in closer proximity than they had been for many a long year. Rachel smelt his body odour, he didn't seem to have washed lately and smelt rank. His eyes seemed to bore right into her; they were cold and hard. Johnny however was slightly unbalanced being so close to his mother and for a few seconds, he remembered her cuddling him and kissing his tears away when he had hurt himself. He banished those thoughts away very quickly.

Nellie's growl became frantic barking and Johnny aimed a kick at her. 'Shut the fuck up or I'll do it for you,' Johnny snarled.

'Leave her alone she's just doing her job.' Rachel got hold of Nellie's collar and dragged the infuriated animal into the little study next to the kitchen and shut the door. She didn't want the old dog hurt.

Johnny strode through into the hallway and threw open the front door revealing another tallish man heavily tattooed and dressed in black motorcycle gear, he too had a beard.

He looked Rachel up and down taking in her arm in a cast then followed Johnny who had gone through into the kitchen.

'Just wanted to see if you've made any progress selling up, Ma, what about giving us a beer and then we can talk business.'

'I haven't any...'

'Liar, YOU TOLD ME LAST TIME YOU HADN'T ANY BEER, BUT YOU HAD, AND SPIRITS TOO!'

Rachel sat down weakly in a chair at the table. 'Stop shouting if you know there's beer, help yourself.' She felt exhausted.

Johnny did just that and he and his mate, Zac, just sat drinking and saying nothing to Rachel. Several times, she tried to speak, but Johnny shushed her and she was too scared to provoke him any further. He meant business.

'Broke your arm then have you?' eventually Johnny said.

'Yes.' Rachel wasn't keen to elaborate.

'Silly bitch. So are you getting on with selling up then? I want my share, maybe even more, you haven't had to keep me for some years after all, saved you a bit, haven't I, not being around, you owe me.'

Gathering all her resolve, Rachel said as firmly as she could, 'I owe you nothing, Johnny, you made your choices when you left and anyway the bank has first call on this place. I owe them first, certainly not you.'

'LIAR!' Johnny brought his fist down in the table with considerable force making Rachel jump out of her skin.

Shaking with fright, Rachel shook her head dumbly.

Johnny got to his feet knocking his chair over as he did so. Putting his face close to Rachel's, he shouted at her, 'LIAR, YOU'LL SELL UP AS SOON

AS YOU CAN, YOU HEAR ME, AND NO EXCUSES. CATTLE, HORSES, HOUSE, EVERYTHING, YOU HEAR ME?'

Rachel nodded not daring to speak; she could hardly not hear him, she thought, as jerking his head at Zac he stomped out of the room. Zac hadn't spoken one word the whole time he'd been there, but as he got to his feet he said, 'If you know what's good for you, you won't cross him.' He had an almost gentle voice but underneath, Rachel felt there was even more menace than Johnny's shouting.

Moments later, she heard the motorbikes roar off.

CHAPTER 12

After they had gone, Rachel sat for a long time alternately shaking and crying. She felt angry, frightened, lonely and she just didn't know what to do or think.

In time, she noticed that it was getting light and poor old Nellie was still shut in the tiny office. She got up shakily on her feet and opened the door. Nellie was panting and seemed distressed, she was very old and had been very upset, as she had known her mistress was in trouble and had wanted to be by her side. She had tried and tried to get out and was exhausted. She now lay on the floor too tired to get up.

'Nellie, oh, Nellie,' Rachel sank down beside her, 'poor old girl, are you alright?'

Though as she said it, Rachel knew she wasn't. She went back to the kitchen and got some water in a bowl. She put it under Nellie's nose. Nellie seemed incapable of sitting up enough to drink, so with difficulty using one arm, Rachel propped her more upright, but Nellie only took a couple of laps at the water. Rachel sat on the floor beside her and let Nellie rest her head in her lap. 'Come on, old girl, you'll be alright soon, come on.' Rachel stroked her pleading with her to get up and feel better, but in her heart, she knew it was too late. She watched the light fade from the old dog's eyes; her heart had finally given out. 'Please don't leave me please, Nellie, don't go.' But as she uttered those words, Rachel knew it was fruitless and Nellie had gone.

Fresh tears rolled down Rachel's face, she felt incapable of moving. She just sat nursing the old dog and remembering all the good times they had had together. Nellie had come as a tiny puppy and almost at once had latched onto Rachel. She wouldn't work for Sam but would do anything Rachel asked of her and had been brilliant working the cattle. More than once, she had alerted Rachel to snakes and Rachel always knew Nellie would lay down her life if necessary, for her. Now in a way she had. Rachel heard the telephone ring but was too emotional to bother about it, she just felt she would nurse Nellie for as long as she could. What did it matter, if she wanted to stay there all day, there was no one to say she shouldn't, no one to tell her to get dressed, eat, drink, do anything, no, she would just sit here with her old dog and sod everything else. Maybe if she sat there long enough, she would die too, then Johnny could have what he wanted. She was so tired of fighting everything. Fighting for Sam, fighting to keep the stud going, fighting to stop Johnny from having the farm and making her life a misery. She leant back against the doorpost and must have dozed off because she woke wondering where she was and what was happening. Then she opened her eyes and found Nellie and it all came flooding back and the tears started again. She didn't hear the door because it was open as Johnny and Zac had left it that way, so when Mike was kneeling on the floor beside her; she was very surprised. For himself, Mike took in the scene and squatted down beside Rachel and putting his arm around her shoulders said, 'Come on, darlin', you can't sit there. Poor old Nellie needs to be put to rest.'

Rachel looked at him with swimming eyes. 'I know,' she whispered, 'but I can't seem to move.'

With his arm firmly around her waist, Mike managed to get Rachel to her feet and averted his eyes to the fact that her nightdress had ridden way up her thighs. He could feel through her dressing gown and nightdress that she was painfully thin and guessed she wasn't bothering to look after herself very well.

He led her into the kitchen, his eyes taking in the beer bottles on the table but said nothing; just put the kettle on to boil and going into the bedroom came back with the doona from the bed and wrapped it round Rachel's shoulders as she was shivering even though it wasn't that cold.

He made her tea with plenty of sugar.

'I don't...'

'You do just now,' he said firmly. She was surprised how it revived her even though she didn't like sugar normally. Mike took his own tea and sat across the table from her not speaking just sitting quietly; he knew she would talk when she was ready.

As she gradually stopped shivering Mike said quietly, 'I think a good hot shower is what you need then we will see to poor old Nellie, yes?'

Rachel nodded and fumbled for the plastic sleeve that she put on her cast when she was showering. She had left it in the kitchen to dry near the stove as it got rather wet the last time. Mike came across and helped her put it on her arm. She was suddenly aware of his proximity and looking up at him seeing the concern for her in his brown eyes. Mike stepped back abruptly. 'There you go,' he said gruffly.

Standing under the shower, which she had as hot as she could stand, Rachel felt a lot better. She was still very upset by the events of the night but felt more able to cope with them. Then she wondered how come Mike had appeared like he had. He was in uniform, so he had to be on duty, why was that then? she thought.

Drying and dressing took some time, but Mike was waiting patiently in the kitchen. 'I hope you don't mind, but I've made toast and coffee. I think we both need it.'

'Smells good, thank you.' Rachel sat down again at the table. 'How come you are here though, Mike? You must be on duty today.'

'Well, I tried to ring you early to say thanks for letting me come out and help but the phone rang out. I figured it was too early for you to be too far away from the house and I got worried, thought maybe something wasn't right.'

Rachel gave him a wan smile. 'I'm so glad you did. I almost gave up in there.' she nodded towards the study door. Then as she looked, she saw Mike had covered Nellie with her old blanket.

She felt the tears threatening again, but Mike distracted her by saying, 'Who were your visitors last night, Rachel; was it Johnny?'

'Umm.' Rachel had a mouthful of toast. 'Yes, he turned up in the middle of the night again with another guy called Zac. He was demanding I got on with selling up, he was... he was—' Rachel stopped speaking. She found it hard to admit how scared she was of him, her own son.

'Describe this Zac to me, if you can.'

Rachel did her best. She described his voice too, how it had sounded gentle but with an underlying menace in it. Until she said the words out loud Rachel didn't realise how profound her fear had been. 'I had shut Nellie in the little study/office place as she was going ballistic and I was afraid they would hurt her, she was too old to be much danger to them but her barking had them on edge. I didn't want her hurt.' The tears returned as Rachel said this last bit.

'What did they actually say Rachel can you remember? Did they threaten you?'

Rachel sat thinking for a minute. 'Not in so many words I suppose, but as he left, Zac said I must do as Johnny says if I know what's good for me.'

'I see; I don't like the sound of that, Rachel, why don't you come back to town and stay with Jane for a little while, till all this has blown over.'

Rachel shook her head. 'It would give them free rein to do whatever they liked out here then, wouldn't it. I think they had been when I was staying in town the other day as it is. I found cigarette butts downstairs; they had helped themselves to stuff out of the freezer.'

Mike looked worried but said nothing more and shortly afterwards, they made their way outside and Mike dug a hole near the big old jacaranda tree where Nellie had liked to lay in the shade. Mike carried Nellie out and laid her gently in the grave. Rachel put an old shirt of her own in with her and when she nodded to Mike, he filled the hole then piled some small rocks on top so nothing would come and disturb the grave.

Afterwards, they went back to the house and Mike again tried to persuade Rachel to come to town, but she refused and reluctantly Mike drove away.

CHAPTER 13

For the next couple of weeks, everything was quiet. Mike took to ringing Rachel every day and, on his days, off would come out to the farm and help out. To start with, she told him not to bother to ring her but soon came to look forward to their telephone conversations and when he came out to help, they fell into an easy friendly companionship. Mike never wasted words and said exactly what he thought. He looked serious most of the time, but when he smiled or laughed his whole demeanour changed, and Rachel detected a wicked sense of fun under his façade. As for Mike, he enjoyed being out on the farm amongst the animals again and he found Rachel a very warm hearted but desperately lonely person. However, she had a very strong will and Mike could tell that she could be very stubborn once she had made up her mind about something. The cows were now calving and every day there was new life in the paddocks. One day, they found a cow in considerable distress; it was unusual as normally they calved easily. They managed to walk her back to the yards; it wasn't far as Rachel always kept the cows near when they were due to calve. Mike rolled up his sleeve and felt inside the cow. 'It's a breech by the feel of it; we're going to have to help this old girl. So with much heaving and twisting, they managed or rather Mike managed to get the calf out. Rubbing it vigorously as it wasn't breathing, Mike looked up at Rachel. 'Sorry mate, looks as though we've lost this one.' Just then the calf twitched and gagged and started to breath much to Rachel and Mike's joy. Later, Rachel reflected on the 'we' that Mike had used. She realised she had started to think the same way. That would never do.

However, she couldn't help but feel this little calf was special and would look out for it whenever she was checking the cattle. She was pleased it was a heifer, which meant it would not be going to the meatworks, at least not yet. '*What am I thinking?*' Rachel said to herself. But then she would rub the little heifer behind her big floppy ears and the little animal would look at her with those huge brown eyes circled by eyelashes that looked like an artist's paintbrush and her heart would melt. '*I must be getting soft in my old age*,' she said to herself.

Rachel was having real trouble sleeping at night and was still very upset about Nellie. She took to sleeping in the old armchair in the kitchen fully clothed because she felt safer that way. However, her sleep was broken, and she often looked and felt exhausted. Mike of course didn't know about her sleeping arrangements nor did anyone else. He did pick up, however, that sleep was something she wasn't getting enough of. Taking the bull by the horns, he spoke to Merv and told him a little of Rachel's problems; though, nothing very personal, just that Rachel looked very tired. Of course, everyone in the small town knew Mike went to help Rachel and gossip was rife, but as they liked and respected both Rachel and Mike, no one was in any way critical.

Then Rachel had to go into town to have her cast taken off her arm. Norma had offered to drive her in as she was going anyway and Rachel, though she had driven around the farm in the ute, was still too ham-fisted to drive safely on the road. Mike had picked up a few supplies for her when he had come out. It was decided that Rachel would stay the night with Jane then Mike would pick her up and take her home the next day. It all went as planned, Rachel enjoyed her trip into town and having other women to talk to. She had known them both a long time and felt she could talk about anything, except Johnny. Johnny had been a taboo subject for years, ever since he first ran away from home. Rachel had told Mike about Johnny that day he had come to the farm alone and got her to admit to the tyre tracks, but she simply couldn't bring herself to talk to anyone else about him. Sleeping in a proper bed gave her a much-needed rest too.

Mike looked at her with approval when he picked her up. She had washed her hair in the shower and normally she would just tie it back, but she was running late so had left it to dry and it framed her face in soft waves. To be free of the cast of her arm made her feel lighter and happier and the good sleep too had helped. She looked better than she had since Nellie died. She had told everyone Nellie had a heart attack and because she was old, no one was surprised and didn't question the circumstances. They chatted away amicably all the way back. Rachel had felt very relaxed until they turned onto the farm drive, then a sudden foreboding took hold of her and she went quiet. Mike glanced at her sensing her change of mood.

'You okay?' he asked.

'Yeah, fine,' was Rachel's brief reply.

It was a windy day and as they drove up, they could see that the front door was banging in the wind. 'I bolted it before I left,' Rachel said pre-empting Mike's enquiry.

As they pulled up, Rachel was half out of the car. 'Rachel, wait!' But Rachel was too quick for him and Mike had to hurry to get to her side. The door had been forced, the bolt was half hanging off, going inside, to start with, there was no obvious sign of disturbance until they got to the kitchen. The remaining beer bottles were strewn about and written across the wall behind the stove was 'DON'T THINK RUNNING AWAY WILL HELP. WE'LL BE BACK.' It was written with something red and going closer Rachel was pretty sure it was one of her lipsticks.

Not stopping in spite of Mike trying to make her wait, she went into to her bedroom. It was the scene of devastation. Her clothes were thrown around the room and many were torn and ripped. Her jewellery box was upturned, and some pieces of costume jewellery were lying on the floor. With a small cry, Rachel knelt and searched frantically amongst the debris. 'My ring, where's my ring?'

Mike knelt down beside her. 'What's it like? There is a ring here,' he said retrieving a ring set with small white stones. Rachel looked then shook her head dumbly.

'No, it's the engagement ring that Sam gave me actually after we were married but that is what it was. It's an emerald, oh God, where is it?'

'Well, let's do this sensibly instead of creating more chaos, we tidy as we go, that way we are more likely to find it. I would like to get some fingerprints done though, so try not to touch other things, only your clothes.' With that, Mike got on the phone.

Rachel sat on the floor and looked around at the mess. Apart from her jewellery box, her make-up and clothes, nothing else seemed damaged she realised, it looked much worse than it was in reality.

In the end, they made three piles of clothes. Those that were no good at all, those Rachel could repair and some that were just thrown but not damaged. Rachel was embarrassed at the thought of Mike helping her sort her underwear, but he left that to her thankfully.

Half an hour or so later, they had everything looking much better when with a cry of delight Rachel who had decided to look under the bed saw her ring. It had rolled away and was lying there waiting to be found, she was so pleased that without thinking she turned and threw her arms around Mike. 'I've found it!'

In those split seconds, Mike stood still then his arms came round her and for a brief second, he hugged her back then pushed her gently and gave her a brief smile. 'Good, now let's make a drink'

Late afternoon a couple of policemen arrived and fussed about taking fingerprints and generally having a good look around for any other evidence, though Mike had been very thorough in his search.

As it was now getting late, Mike was worried about leaving Rachel and was racking his brains about the best thing to do. He had repaired the door and double-checked all the windows and other doors that led off the veranda.

Rachel too was worried though she tried to hide it. 'Do you want a bite to eat before you head off?' she said.

They both knew it was a delaying tactic and Mike shook his head, he had things he needed to do, some of them important. He had not meant to be out at the farm for as long as he had been, as it was.

CHAPTER 14

Gradually over the next few weeks, Rachel managed to put these events behind her, she had plenty to do to keep her occupied and tried not to go to bed until she was completely exhausted. However, she only slept lightly and spasmodically so she was constantly tired. Mike came out to help whenever he could and the two of them fell into an easy relationship. By an unspoken pact they kept everything on an impersonal level; though, Mike was worried about Rachel, she looked so tired and care worn; however, he thought it best to keep quiet.

Spring marched on, then one day Mike brought up the fact it would be Christmas in just over three-weeks' time. Rachel shuddered; she was dreading it, not only because of Sam dying on Boxing Day but the prospect of spending the day alone. Sam's mother and sisters were all adamant they didn't want to come out to the farm, it would be too upsetting and Rachel's father Fred was getting over a hip replacement, which hadn't gone to plan. Rachel's brother Geoff and his wife Liz, who lived near Fred, felt they shouldn't make the long drive south and leave him. They lived north of Cairns and grew sugar cane. Both sets of family had asked Rachel to go to them, but she felt she had to stay and somehow guard the farm, metaphorically at least. The prospect of the day alone wasn't something Rachel was looking forward to, but then she reminded herself it was just a day like any other. More the fact that it was family time for so many that made her feel so lost.

'Penny for them, what do you do at Christmas then, Rachel?' Mike interrupted her thoughts.

'Oh, nothing much, Sam dying last Christmas has made it take on a whole new meaning I guess.'

'Sorry; yes, it would have done. I'm driving to Brisbane to see the kids, then hopefully they will be out to stay with me for a few days at New Year.'

Rachel felt a stab of jealousy, how she would love to have some grand children around or any children really, for her a big part of Christmas was for children.

Mike looked down scrapping his boot back and forth in the dusty soil. 'I wondered if you would consider having a picnic out at the Wagtails Dam on Boxing Day?'

Rachel sucked in her breath. Wagtails Dam, so called because there seemed more wagtails out there than anywhere, was also the place where most of the little town would head to that day. There were lots of loosely organised events going on, sausage sizzles, hunting for small presents for the little kids, songs around the campfire later in the day, and storytelling. Lots of different and fun things going on. Sam and herself had been a few times over the years, it was a good community activity to go to. But the gossips would be out too. It was one thing Mike coming out to help her and quite another to be seen as a couple at the Wagtails Dam knees up.

'Sorry, Mike, it's a lovely thought, but I don't think it's a good idea.'

Mike looked hard at her. 'Is that because you are worried about what people might say, you can't bear the thought of spending the day with me socially or you just don't like the whole idea?'

Rachel was by now really squirming mentally. 'I have been in the past. It's fun, but as you say it will make the gossips gossip like mad. I would be happy to spend the day in your company not working, but really it's not a good idea.'

Mike looked disappointed but saying nothing more went back to replacing some of the rails in the cattle yards.

Rachel nearly changed her mind but kept to her resolve, another thing she told herself, Mike was five or six years younger than her at least, he was just being kind and she didn't want to go to the picnic with him because he pitied her.

First Jane then Norma both rang to invite her for Christmas Day, but she refused saying there was too much to do but really, she didn't want to go, she wasn't a charity case!

Again, they were disappointed but didn't push it; they knew her too well.

On Christmas day when Rachel woke, she knew it was going to be a very hot one. The days leading up to it had been very humid and today felt very sticky already. Rachel got out of bed deciding she needed to get all the jobs done as early as possible so she would avoid working in the heat of the day.

She told herself it was a normal day and while she was working this theory was good but as the heat rose, she retreated to the house and that is when she found it harder to cope. Also, at the back of her mind, Johnny loomed large. She went through to the rarely used sitting room and got out a large photo album that was there. She sat down with a glass of water and took time looking through the album. It was all before Johnny's accident and some of the pictures were so cute it made her weep, wherever had the dear little blonde boy gone. With his cheeky grin and his chubby arms held out to her in one photo that Sam must have taken, he looked like everyone's dream child. It won't do, she decided sitting here being maudlin; she closed the book with a snap and as she did so a large photo, that must have been a blow up from the one she had been looking at, fell out. Picking it up she put it to one side, she would find a frame for it then she would remember the good times, not the unhappy ones.

Later, she took a series of phone calls from family; hers and Sam's, they were all rather stilted though as none of them knew what to say.

Late afternoon, first Jane then Norma rang then one or two others from town who always looked out for her. She was very touched but wasn't relaxed talking to any of them, partly because she felt she had to pretend that it was better than it really was.

She had just stepped out of the shower pre-bedtime when the phone rang again. She didn't know whether to answer it or not, she was afraid it was Johnny or one of his crew.

She let it ring longer than normal but finally decided to answer it. 'Hello,' she said tentatively.

'Hi, Rachel, how's things, you okay? Got through the day alright?'

Because Mike hadn't skirted round the subject of a lonely day or pretended everything was alright, Rachel found she could be frank too and let her feelings show. 'I'm okay but had better days I admit, get tomorrow over and I'll be fine, how about you, are you back yet?'

'The kids were pleased to see me but apart from that it was a pretty shitty day. I've just stopped for a comfort break and thought I'd check in. Anyway, look after yourself, see ya.' And he was gone before Rachel could reply, she was getting used to his abrupt manner now though and got into bed feeling better than she had all day.

She slept well for the first half of the night but woke at 2am and couldn't get back to sleep. She kept hearing noises, but they were nothing really, most of it being her overactive mind. Finally, as the sun was coming up, she fell into a proper sleep again and with-it vivid dreams. Afterwards, she couldn't quite recall them, but they involved Mike and Johnny and she woke with her heart racing and a feeling of dread in her chest.

CHAPTER 15

When she finally got herself together it was late, by her standards anyway and it was already very hot. '*The good thing about Wagtails Dam was it was a lovely place to swim*,' she thought to herself as, having checked the windmills nearby and collected the eggs and all her normal jobs, she was wet through, the sweat trickling down her legs. She was wearing shorts today instead of her jeans, which is what she mostly wore at home. They were a bit tatty but who cared? There was no one to see.

There was the sound of an engine and a cloud of dust coming up her road. '*Oh God, don't let it be Johnny*,' she thought as she watched it come closer. It wasn't, it was Mike.

'Hi there, Rachel, I need you to come with me ASAP, I need you to look at some mug shots of the guy that was with Johnny.'

'What now, on Boxing Day, now?'

'Yes, if you don't mind it's important.'

Rachel was mystified, why did Mike want her to go this minute, surely, it could wait, but as she started to argue, Mike seemed to get more agitated. 'Change if you must,' he said to her objection, 'but hurry up, you look fine to me.'

Rachel went indoors and rummaging around found another pair of cleaner slightly smarter shorts, brushed her hair and went back out. As she turned to lock the door, Mike said, 'Don't worry about that I don't think anyone will bother today, just come woman, will you?'

Rachel was surprised by this and because it seemed so silly, she gave in and got into his ute beside him. He wasn't in uniform, so it was overtime she guessed. Maybe he had something else he wanted to do today hence all the hurry.

Instead of turning towards town however when they reached the road, Mike turned in the opposite direction. 'Where are you going Mike, it's the wrong way.'

'Oh, so it is, never mind we'll take the scenic route.'

'It's about 50 kilometres further and I thought you were in a hurry.'

'Well, never mind, this road joins the road to town I've been told so now we're on it we'll go this way. You can show me, I don't think I've been along here before.'

'You must have done, Mike what's going on?' Rachel began to feel alarmed.

Mike looked across at her and smiled. 'Trust me please, Rachel, you do trust me, don't you?'

Feeling even more flummoxed now Rachel nodded. 'I suppose so.'

They drove for some distance in comparative silence, just the odd remark about things they saw as they passed by. Rachel didn't feel like talking and Mike seemed rather distracted. Eventually, a turning came up that would lead them back to the normal way to town though nearer to Rachel's place than town.

As they turned here Rachel said, 'You might have carried on if we're going to town, this takes us back on ourselves.'

'Oh, does it?'

Rachel by this time was feeling very suspicious of Mike, what on earth was he up to? However, though she felt uncertain, she also realised she wasn't afraid or worried, more mystified than anything.

Before long they were turning back into her gravel drive, Rachel still kept quiet guessing that she would soon know what was going on. As they crested the small hill and started down towards the house, Rachel could see three cars parked out the front of her house. 'Mike!'

Mike grinned at her. 'It's okay just wait and see.' They drew up in front by the veranda steps and no sooner had they then the front door flew open and Sid, Norma, Jane, Bob and their two girls Beth and Angie all came down the steps saying 'Happy Christmas'. Rachel was dumbfounded and sat in the car with an expression of disbelief on her face. Mike who had got out came round to her side and gently hauled her to her feet. The others then all gathered round her giving her hugs and wishing her a happy belated

Christmas all over again. Rachel's throat was too closed with unshed tears to say anything, she just kept nodding with her eyes swimming with tears, she felt over-whelmed.

They led her through the house to the back where the barbeque, which she hadn't used for a long time, had been cleaned and was now heaped with steak and sausages. They had got the trestle out of the shed and that was almost groaning with food on the veranda.

'Come on, let's eat. We were wondering if you'd got lost,' Sid said as he looked longingly at the food. 'It's all ready to go.'

'I had the devil's own job to persuade her to come with me, then she took ages to get ready,' Mike said smiling at Rachel.

Rachel swallowed the lump in her throat. 'I wasn't aware policemen could be so devious,' she retorted.

Mike was busy heaping a plate with food and didn't answer but plonked it in front of her. 'Eat,' he commanded.

Rachel surprised herself by the amount of food she managed to eat. In fact, everybody consumed a lot of food and not a small amount of wine and beer.

Sid announced he was driving across country and wouldn't be going on the road at all. There was a gate between the two, which hadn't been used much lately, but it had always been handy. Jane wasn't drinking so they didn't have a problem. Mike had a beer at the beginning and a glass of wine later. Norma, Rachel and Bob had no such worries and it was the most Rachel had drunk for a very long time.

Halfway through the proceedings, she stood up and banged a spoon down on the table loudly. 'I just want to thank you all for all this. It's amazing of you all. Whose idea was it? Whoever it was I shall never be able, be able...' Then the tears came, she couldn't help it.

Norma, who was nearest, put her arms round her. She was a bit choked up too as they that had known Sam all were. 'It's okay, Rach, we did it for you and for Sam too, maybe he is looking down and raising a glass as well. We all loved him, he was a great guy, and this is a kind of memorial to him as well as a 'cheer up Rachel day'.'

Rachel hugged her back saying, 'Thank you, all of you.'

With throats clearing gruffly, the men folk started to talk about the weather, and everyone did their best to get back to being light hearted.

Twenty minutes later, they were all back laughing and talking. Bob who had an old guitar, which he could play reasonably well, started to strum away and sing. Now Bob couldn't sing a note, he was always off key, but it made everybody roll around in fits of laughter especially his daughters who were mortified by their father's behaviour, but at the same time could see the funny side of it. The party became quite raucous, so much so that they didn't hear the motor bike roaring up and were startled by someone shouting to Rachel, 'CELEBRATING THE OLD MAN'S DEATH I SEE, MIND IF I JOIN IN?'

There was complete silence for several moments as Johnny walked over to the table and picked up a beer, then he turned and smirking at all the stunned faces said, 'Well, Ma, who are these sheilas then?' looking at Beth and Angie, 'I wouldn't mind a piece of these two.'

Rachel found her voice then, 'Get out of here Johnny, you're not welcome now or ever, get out!' As she said this she took a step towards him, anger blazing in her eyes.

Johnny laughed, a hollow sound. 'You gonna make me, Ma, in front of all these people, your own flesh and blood, at Christmas, how about the season of goodwill? You don't seem to have much of that.'

Rachel hesitated then, was she being unreasonable? He was her son after all, however as she wavered, Sid stepped in 'You heard your mother, you're not welcome, get on your bike and go.'

Sid was as tall as Johnny and very fit, for a second it looked as if Johnny was going to throw a punch, but in the end he laughed mirthlessly. 'Silly old fool, Sid Newberry, you'll regret this.' With a single movement, he swept his arm over the table and sent bottles and plates flying. He then stopped at the corner of the house saying, 'See ya, Ma.' and was gone.

All eyes turned to Mike who had kept still and silent throughout all this. 'Are you going after him, Mike?' said Sid.

To everyone's surprise, Mike shook his head. 'Nah, do more harm than good, come on let's clear this mess up.'

Still feeling shocked and upset, everyone helped clear up then Jane made tea and coffee and before long, they were saying their goodbyes.

CHAPTER 16

They all worried about leaving Rachel, but she said she was sure Johnny wouldn't come back that day. Mike, however, lingered on.

'Rachel, I'm sorry I kept to the background when Johnny appeared, I didn't think it would do for him to see a policeman here or come to that a single male. He might think I am trying to muscle in and that might make him more violent and unpredictable. So, I'm sorry if it's made me look a bit weak, but I was doing what I thought was best.'

Rachel smiled tiredly. 'It's okay, Mike, I don't think he saw you, really he was too busy being obnoxious.'

Mike gave her one of his rare smiles. 'Are you going to be okay? Do you want me to hang around a bit longer?'

Rachel shook her head. 'I'll be fine, thanks, really.'

Still Mike hesitated then swiftly he bent forward and very gently kissed her on the lips. 'Take care.' And he was gone, jumping in his ute and driving away without a backwards glance.

Rachel stood rooted to the spot until he had long gone, and the dust had settled. Her heart was thumping away in her chest and her head was in a whirl. She couldn't deny to herself that she was attracted to him, he wasn't handsome in the accepted sense but when he smiled it made her heart leap. Also, he was so kind and caring, she felt safe and unafraid when he was around. She loved the way his warm brown eyes twinkled when he said something silly to wind her up as he would sometimes. Then she would know she was being gently teased. Much like Sam used to do, but Sam could never keep a straight face for long whereas Mike could.

She pulled herself together, it was only a year ago today that Sam had died and anyway Mike was several years younger than her and married.

For the next few days, Rachel was very jumpy but nothing untoward happened, then on New Year's Eve, Mike rang. He hadn't been in contact since Boxing Day, the others had all spoken to her on the phone and Rachel was guessing that Mike regretted the kiss, fleeting though it was. Without preamble Mike said, 'Rachel, hello, I have my kids staying and wondered if we could all come out to the farm tomorrow. The kids don't know anything much about the countryside and have never been on a farm before.'

'Yes, Mike, that's fine.'

As usual before Rachel could ask what time or anything he said, 'Happy New Year, thanks.' And he put the phone down.

Rachel gave a wry smile. she was getting used to his telephone manner now.

Rachel sat thinking for a few minutes then got into top gear. She made cookies and muffins, she cleaned and polished and finally sat down realising that it was getting dark and she still had jobs to do outside. Her mind had been in an excited whirl all day; she was so looking forward to tomorrow.

The next morning though, she was inexplicably nervous. It's silly, she told herself, they are just two young children, why does it matter so much, but she couldn't quell the butterflies in her stomach.

She had only just finished her breakfast when she heard Mike's ute coming and was out on the veranda as it drew up. A small girl then an even smaller boy got tentatively out of the car. Both were blonde and serious looking but as Rachel got closer, she could see that Emma the little girl had Mike's dark brown eyes whereas Ben had blue eyes.

Rachel squatted down in front of them and held out her hand, she could see they were a mixture of excited and nervous. 'Hello, you must be Ben and you are Emma?' she said, deliberately getting their names the wrong way round.

The children stared at her then Emma broke into a delighted giggle. 'Silly, I'm Emma and this is Ben.'

Rachel pretended to be very surprised by this. 'Are you sure?'

Ben by now had got over his shyness a little and said loudly, 'I'm Ben and she's known as Em.'

Rachel again pretended to be confused and said, 'I'm Barbara, known as Boo, though sometimes called Rachel or Rach.'

Mike stood watching this exchange with a grin on his face and then winking at Rachel said, 'Well, Mrs BOORACH, shall we go in or are we standing out here all day?' So they all walked towards the house and before long, the children were tucking into muffins and chocolate milk while Mike and Rachel had a coffee.

Rachel watched the children take in their surrounds as they munched away. Mike and she exchanged a few words and Rachel told him what she thought the children might like to see and do.

Then Emma said, 'Is your surname really Mrs Boorach?'

Mike and Rachel then burst out laughing. 'No sweetheart, of course not, it's your dad being cheeky, my name is Rachel and that is what you can call me okay?'

When the children had finished their morning tea or smoko as Rachel told them it was called out there, they all went outside and Rachel gave each of them a small plastic container with some chook food in it and took them to the run where the chooks were kept. Em was a bit afraid of the hens to start with, as they rushed towards her looking for their grain. After a few minutes though, she relaxed when she understood they wouldn't hurt her. They then collected the eggs and were fascinated to find that at least two of them were still warm. 'That's because they have only just been laid,' said Rachel.

'Laid, what does that mean?' Ben looked mystified.

'Well, the hens have eggs inside them and then they lay them,' Rachel explained.

'You mean they lie down and when they get up there is an egg there? But how does it get out of them?'

At this point, Emma decided to tell her baby brother what she had already worked out.

'They come out of their bottoms, silly,' she said.

Ben wasn't at all impressed with this and started to argue with his sister over it. Rachel soon distracted them by taking them to the veggie patch and getting them to help her pick some tomatoes and beans.

A little later, she took them to see the cattle that were nearest. At this point, she wandered around until she came on her special calf and the children were delighted when the little animal came up to them and actually wanted them to scratch her behind her ears. 'Remember this one, Mike?' Rachel looked at him and smiled.

'I do, is that the one that was a breech?'

'Yes, she a fine girl now aren't you little one?'

'What's her name?' Ben wanted to know and finding out she hadn't got one the children came up with all sorts of improbable names. This led to an argument. So, to distract them Rachel took them to see Spot, then saddled the old horse up and led them in turn around the yard. All this time Mike watched from the sidelines quietly.

Then they went in and Rachel gave them homemade pizza for lunch. She had assembled them first thing, so all she had to do was check they both ate the toppings then pop them into the oven.

The children tucked in hungrily, they had ice cream afterwards, again homemade.

Mike and Rachel of course joined the children, and both watched with amusement at the children's appetites.

'Can we go out and play now please,' asked Em when they had finished.

'Yes but collect your plates up and put them in the sink,' said Mike. 'And watch out for snakes,' he added as minutes later the children made for the door.

Rachel got to her feet and silently they cleared and washed up. Neither said a word, they were both aware of how much this visit meant for the children and for Rachel too.

When they had finished and Rachel was drying her hands, Mike put his hand on her shoulder and turned her to face him. 'I just want to say thank you, Rachel, the kids have had the best time and so have I. It's been a special day.'

Rachel was very aware of him and his hand still on her shoulder, taking a deep breath she said, 'It has been special and not over yet, let's take the kids down to the creek. There is a swimming hole we could go to, what do you think?'

'Sure, why not, I—' Mike didn't say more as the kids came bursting back in.

'Come on Daddy, we want to explore more, that is, can we Rachel?'

Shortly afterwards, they were all crammed into Rachel's ute heading down to the creek. When they got to the paddock that the creek ran through, Rachel couldn't supress a small shudder. Mike looked at her and reaching across touched her shoulder saying, 'You okay honey?'

'Yep, we are going the other way.'

'What other way?' the children chorused. Of course, Mike knew what Rachel meant but just said, 'We are going left instead of right.'

They had a ball down at the swimming hole. It was just deep enough for the children to swim safely, and Mike and Rachel paddled and watched them enjoy themselves. Rachel had brought drinks and biscuits, which they consumed before heading back.

It was getting late by the time they got back to the house so Mike said he would go straight home. The children were very quiet, and Rachel guessed they would be asleep before they got back.

'Please can we come again? Please Daddy, Rachel?' Em pleaded as she scrambled into her father's car.

Rachel who had just found herself wetly kissed by Ben said she'd love them to come again. Emma got out of the car again and put her little arms around Rachel's waist. 'Thank you Rachel, for an awesome day and for saying we can come back. It is the best day of my life!'

Mike gave one of his rare smiles. 'The day after tomorrow if that suits you, Rach, would that be okay?'

'Like Ben and Em just said, awesome,' Rachel replied. Mike touched her briefly on the shoulder. 'Thanks mate,' he said quietly getting into the car.

Rachel stood waving and watched until the swirl of dust had disappeared in the gathering gloom.

She slept well that night better than she had at home for a long time and felt almost light-hearted the next morning as she went about her jobs.

CHAPTER 17

Later that day though, her peace was shattered as she could hear a motor bike. Listening hard she could hear several and they were coming her way. She stood waiting for them to come over the rise, but they didn't, they seemed to go to the left. Then she twigged where they were going. When the property was first settled, it was a sheep station not cattle and the old shearing shed, and ruined homestead were on a track some distance away from the present house. The present house itself was eighty years old so the old house was nothing more than a ruin, the shearing shed and a few other buildings weren't that bad; however, as Sam and his father before him had used them for all sorts of things over the years. It was sometime since this had been the case though and they were looking rather dilapidated.

Rachel stood wondering what to do and what if it was Johnny and why was he going there? She didn't have to wait long however, before she heard the bikes coming closer. They cut across the home paddock and left the gate swinging. The heifers she had kept back spooked and huddled together near a small cluster of trees.

Anger overrode her fear, and she stormed across toward Johnny and the six of his friends he had with him.

Johnny stopped his bike and sat astride it, grinning at her as she approached. 'What the hell are you doing, you know better than to leave gates open, did you shut the other one the other side?'

Johnny just grinned wider than ever then turning to the others said, 'See what I have to put up with from the old woman, that's why I don't live with her, right old nag.'

The others just nodded; they all had their helmets on, only Johnny had taken his off. Rachel walked past him to shut the gate. Johnny swung his bike into her path.

'Just listen to me, Ma, time is running out. I want you out of here. I'll take over now. Just pack up and leave.'

Rachel stared at him. 'What are you talking about? You don't want the farm; you've made that very clear. It's my home. I'm not leaving.'

'We'll see about that, won't we, lads?'

Rachel's fear returned. 'What do you mean?'

Johnny sat smirking. 'I'm a reasonable man, Ma, even though you don't think so. I'll give you two months to sell the cattle and clear out. I don't care what any fancy lawyers may say I'm claiming it, all of it, you understand?'

'What if I don't?'

'You will, Ma, you will believe me you'll be pleased to leave if you drive me too far. The boys here can be very persuasive and so CAN I.'

Rachel physically jumped as he shouted the last two words at her.

Suddenly, he fired his bike up and rode round and round her in a circle then the others joined in. The dust was choking and also blinded her, shaking with fright, all she could do was stand still and wait till it was over. Then suddenly they all peeled away and took off up the track towards the road. Only Johnny remained. He took his helmet off once more and said, 'That was nothing, you hear me, nothing.' Then he too was gone.

Automatically, Rachel went and shut the gate. Her heart was hammering in her chest and then she started to shake, on wobbly legs she made it back to the house and dragging herself up the veranda steps she collapsed into the old cane chair and shut her eyes. She tried to control her breathing as she found she was almost panting. Gradually, her heart rate slowed down, and she stopped shaking, she was covered with dust, it was in her hair, her clothes, everywhere.

She got to her feet and on weak legs went through to the bedroom. She peeled off her clothes and got into the shower. For a long time, she just let the water run over her until finally, she felt energised enough to shampoo her hair and wash all the dust and grime away.

Returning to the kitchen, she made herself a strong cup of coffee then sat thinking over what had happened. She resolved to go to the police but shrank from involving Mike. She didn't know why, but instinctively she wanted to keep him out of it. He was too close to her, and if Johnny got wind of their friendship, it might make matters worse. Having made that decision she then thought maybe going to see her lawyer might be better, after all Johnny hadn't done anything criminal, at least not that she knew of.

Later, she was almost afraid to go out to shut the chickens up and feed the dogs and check on her old horse. She got Sam's gun to take with her, though she knew she'd never use it against a human and she only had about three cartridges left, anyway. However, it felt better having it with her and she hurried doing her jobs and was back in the house very quickly. Then she went round making sure every window and door was secure. She picked the phone up and gave a sigh of relief that there was a dial tone.

She drew all the blinds she could, but for a time sat in the dark, afraid to put on the light and make it obvious that she was home. She knew it was silly as her car was out the front, but in some ways, the dark felt safer.

Eventually, she pulled herself together again and putting on the lights made herself a light supper. She didn't feel like eating but knew she must. Once it was bedtime, she got a blanket from her bedroom and sat in the chair in the kitchen. She was too fearful to go to bed.

Of course, she only catnapped all night and by dawn, she felt exhausted, but as Mike and the children were coming out, she attempted to wake up and get ready for the day.

By the time the children and Mike arrived, she was feeling much better; she had showered and changed and for once left her hair loose and even put on a smudge of lipstick. She didn't really know why she was doing this but just wanted to feel better and anyway she already knew she had fallen for Mike's kids; they were so sweet. She had picked up from what they had said that Mike's wife had a new man in her life that they didn't like, and in a strange way she wanted to protect them. 'Silly girl,' she said to herself, 'they are nothing to do with you.'

They were much later arriving this time, and Rachel had got very anxious waiting for them. When at last they drew up, she was down the veranda steps and opening the children's door saying, 'I was getting so worried, I thought you weren't coming.'

Mike looked at her oddly. He could see the strain on her face even though she had tried to cover it up.

'What's up, Rach? You are overreacting a bit, aren't you, what's wrong?'

Determined not to tell him about her visitors, Rachel gave what she hoped was a winning smile. 'Nothing, why would there be, come along you two, who is going to find the first egg?'

The children of course responded with great excitement and ran off towards the chicken run.

Mike fell into step with her as she followed them. 'Rachel, I know you well enough by now to tell when something is wrong, please tell me. Don't you trust me?'

Rachel stopped in her tracks and turned slowly to face him. 'Yes, of course

I trust you, Mike, but really you have enough of your own problems to keep you busy without mine.'

Mike gently picked up her hand in his and looking down at it said, 'Rachel, please tell me. I don't like to see you unhappy and if you don't tell me, I shall just be imagining the worst. It's Johnny, isn't it?'

She gently withdrew her hand and nodded, unable suddenly to speak. Just then, the children came running back both holding the handle of the egg basket between them. 'I was first!'

'No, I was!' A big argument erupted and Rachel could put her emotions aside and even forgot about them in the ensuing few hours. Mike said nothing more as he was aware that Rachel won't say anything in front of the children, not that he wanted her too.

They had a very similar morning to the time before, though this time the children were more confident and outgoing. Rachel teased them gently too, and they all played hide and seek; though, Mike and Rachel warned them against places where spiders or snakes might be.

After lunch, Mike told the children to go and play outside for a bit and they would join them soon. Rachel looked at him sharply she guessed what was coming.

'Now, please tell me what's up.' He was sitting across the table from her and again picked up her hand that was lying on the table.

Rachel looked up into his warm brown eyes and her resolve not to say anything crumbled. Fighting to keep control of her tears she said, 'Yes, Johnny was here with about six others, he said he'd give me two months then he is taking over whether I like it or not or whatever the law says, I suppose. He said, he said...' Rachel couldn't continue, she just shook her head.

Mike stroked her hand, his fingers warm and reassuring. 'Did they do anything, honey?'

'They all rode round and round me and covered me in dust. Then they rode off except Johnny, who threatened me again, but I can't really remember what he said, I was too upset.'

Mike fished his handkerchief out of his pocket. 'I saw motor bike tracks in places in the dust. I guessed you'd had visitors. Why don't you come to town and stay with Jane a few days until you feel a little better?'

Rachel shook her head. 'It makes it harder when I come back then.' She looked at Mike with swimming eyes. 'What shall I do Mike, I didn't want to involve you, it's not fair on you and I'm so scared.'

'We'll think of something,' as he said this the children came rushing into the room.

'We've found a spiky thing,' said Ben.

'An echidna, silly,' said Em. 'Come and see please, at least I think that is what it is.' She felt doubtful suddenly.

The two adults got to their feet and followed the children outside, Mike took Rachel's hand and gave it a brief squeeze as they went. It was reassuring.

Having looked in vain for 'Mr Spikey' as Ben called him, the children wanted to know what they could do next. Rachel then had a brainwave and the next two hours Mike and herself got busy making up a swing for the children. There was an ancient Port Jackson Fig near the back of the house which, with its low branches and spreading habit, made it ideal for a swing. Two swings in the end. Rachel found a sturdy rope for one and a chain for the other while Mike fashioned wooden seats for the children. Rachel was afraid they might get splinters in their bottoms so she found some old cushions that had been used for loungers outside and sometime later, the children were swinging away happily.

There was an old wooden seat out there near the veggie patch and Mike and Rachel both went to sit down and watch the children enjoy the fruits of their labour. They both sat simultaneously and the next moment, they were both sitting on the ground. The bench had given up the ghost, but it had looked alright from the outside. Rachel got the giggles and Mike too laughed, but not so much as the children who laughed until they were crying.

Mike got to his feet first and hauled Rachel up. 'That was so funny, Daddy,' called Em. 'Pity the bench is broken; you could do it again.'

'Are you alright, Rach? Not hurt?'

Rachel wiped tears of laughter from her eyes.

'No, not at all, it's good to laugh at something.'

Glancing across at the children, Mike said in a low voice, 'Please come into town and stay with Jane tonight until we work out what's best to do, just one night, what do you say?'

Rachel thought for a moment, then nodded. 'I must admit I feel so scared and isolated, and I didn't sleep last night, not really, so yes I'll ring Jane now.'

CHAPTER 18

Jane was more than happy for Rachel to come and stay and even persuaded her to come for two nights, as the second night there was to be a fundraising trivia night at the pub. The local C.W.A. building needed repairs and also a fresh coat of paint, so after rejecting different ideas a trivia night it was to be. Sam and Rachel used to go to as many social events as they could when they were younger, but after Johnny became difficult, they had stopped socialising so much. The last couple of years Rachel hadn't gone to anything social at all, first while Sam was ill and now, she hadn't been inclined to. Maybe she would get back into it she thought. Then she thought about Johnny, maybe not, who knew what would happen next. Norma was happy to go across to feed the dogs the next day and longer if Rachel wanted her to. Rachel impressed on her it would only be the two nights though; she was afraid the longer she was away the harder it would be to go back.

So, after she had waved Mike and the children off, Rachel set about getting a few things together for her short break.

The children had clung to her before they left, as in a couple of days they were going back to their mother in Brisbane. They had both got upset saying goodbye, but Rachel told them she would treat them to morning tea at the bakery the next day so they went off happily. Mike too as he was relieved Rachel was going to Jane's.

Driving into town as the sun set, she was taken in with the beauty of the surrounding countryside. Most times, she didn't notice but not having to hurry too much and being in a reflective mood she was more aware of the indigo sky with few orange streaks across it where the sun had set. The tall gums with their pale trunks and branches, cattle silhouetted against the darkening landscape, the sky reflected in a large dam like a huge mirror, she sighed it was all so beautiful and peaceful, why couldn't life be like that?

Jane welcomed her with open arms. 'I have been worrying about you ever since Johnny turned up on Boxing Day. I'm so glad you've come to stay. You know you are welcome as long as you want, don't you?'

Rachel's resolve not to cry if Jane was kind crumbled, she nodded, eyes filling with those ever-present tears. 'I'm sorry.' She sniffed. 'I don't know what the matter with me is I keep crying over nothing.'

'That isn't true, my love, you have had the most horrible time lately and Johnny turning up is the last thing you need right now.'

Rachel nodded, she agreed with that fervently.

Later when they had eaten dinner and were sitting around the table before clearing up, Rachel told Bob and Jane about Mike's children and what they had got up to. She didn't notice the look that passed between her friends, but Jane said to Bob later that night she thought Rachel looked happier relating those stories than anything had made her lately. Bob pointed out that Rachel was a frustrated mother, grandmother, all those things that make having children a delight that had been denied her.

'Maybe Mike's children could fill the gap if her and Mike get together,' he said. Jane shook her head. She had guessed her friend was smitten by Mike, but he was married and younger and Jane couldn't see it happening.

CHAPTER 19

The next morning two, very excited children were waiting for Rachel as she had said she would pick them up. Mike had rented a small cottage on the edge of town and the children were waiting at the gate as Rachel drove up. She had been going to walk, but it was exceedingly hot so she had decided to drive instead.

'Hello, you two, where's your Dad, is he coming?' she asked.

Em shook her head. 'No, he says he has some police work to do, he said he'll see you later.'

Rachel was taken aback at how disappointed she felt by this. She realised she had been looking forward to spending more time with Mike than she was aware she wanted to.

'Right, we'll go to the park first, shall we, then find some morning tea.'

'Okay, we've been to the park before with Dad but that's okay,' Em said.

'Is there anything else you'd like to do then?'

'What's that big truck?' Ben pointed to an enormous truck that was just pulling up in the high street.

'That's a mobile library, it comes twice a month,' said Rachel.

'Cool, can we go and look?' said Em.

'Please can we?' Ben joined in.

'Yes, if you want, but we may have to wait a few minutes while they get organised, but yes we can look inside if you want.'

Rachel was so surprised by their request she rather muffed her reply. She assumed that the children would be into computer games and not be interested in books. So, a short time later, she was even more surprised to find herself surrounded by books and two excited children who thought a mobile library was far more interesting than one in a building.

There was a tiny table up one end with three little chairs and before Rachel had got her thoughts together, Em and Ben were seated at the table both looking at books they had found. Rachel hovered nearby, as Johnny had never been interested in books nor really had Sam. Although she had always liked to read, the mobile library wasn't somewhere she had visited. Also, she was hardly ever in town at the same time as the library so sometimes she would go to the op shop and pick something up.

The woman in charge asked Rachel if the children wanted to borrow anything or just sit there and read.

'Well, they are going home tomorrow so can we all just stay here for a bit?' Rachel said.

'Of course, my name is Emily, pleased to meet you, are you and your grandchildren new to the area?'

Rachel was mortified, her GRANDCHILDREN?! Did she look that old? Then thinking about it she supposed she was old enough. Oh god, what a shock. New to the area, she had lived hereabouts for nearly thirty years, how dare this younger upstart make these assumptions.

Just as she was about to make a tart reply she caught sight of herself in the reflection of some glass-fronted shelves in front of her. She was looking exhausted, her hair was scraped back willy-nilly, she was dressed in daggy old clothes; she looked little better than down and out! She had let herself go and had given up caring how she looked, indeed caring about many things. Staying one-step ahead of Johnny seemed her only focus on life at late. Time to stop and refocus. She would start today!

They ended up spending an entire hour in there, the children's delight in the whole place was infectious and Rachel found herself actually joining the library, something she had never done before. She borrowed a couple of books and was very surprised to find that she could have them an entire month before returning them.

They walked back down the road towards the bakery where Rachel thought they would have morning tea. The library had been air-conditioned, and it was very hot outside. Both children were hot and bothered by the time they got to the bakery, so it was water then cold milkshakes for them. Rachel had an iced chocolate and they all had a brownie each, but neither child could finish theirs, so Rachel wrapped them in serviettes so they could eat them later. Just as they were leaving, a big motorbike pulled into the kerb nearby. Rachel shrank back, was it Johnny or one of his friends, but when the guy got off and took his helmet off Rachel didn't think she had seen him before. He wasn't any taller than her but had a mass of dark curly hair, which was long. He was very good looking too and as he glanced in their direction; Rachel saw dancing blue eyes that looked full of mischief. By this time, the children were waiting for Rachel to get into the car and take them back, so she hurried on to catch up to them. She had to admit the man intrigued her, though.

Driving towards the edge of town, she stopped suddenly and told the children to sit still; she popped into the only hairdressers in town and asked Gemma the hairdresser if she could come back later for a trim.

'I'm fully booked, Rach, sorry,' Gemma said. Then seeing the disappointment on Rachel's face said, 'Okay, come back at five thirty I'll give you a trim then, will you still be in town then?'

'Yes, not going back until tomorrow, thanks, Gemma, you're a star.' Rachel almost did a little dance as she left the shop. Then having second thoughts, she went back and asked Gemma if she could go the next day instead before she went home. It would give her longer as she decided to have more than a trim.

When they got to the cottage, the children rushed in front of Rachel shouting for their father in great excitement.

Mike met them on the veranda. 'Whoa, what's all the fuss, where's the fire?'

Both children were talking at once and shouting each other down, telling him about the mobile library and how awesome it was. Finally, they ran out of steam. Mike looked at Rachel and winked. 'You've had a pretty boring morning then,' he said. That started them off all over again. Then Mike told them to go and tidy their rooms and start packing their things away as they were leaving to go back to Brisbane the next day. That quietened them down considerably, and they shuffled off to do as their dad had said.

Mike indicated that Rachel take a seat, which she did. 'What would you like to drink?'

'Just some nice cold water, thank you,' she said, settling herself down.

'I am sorry not to be coming this evening. I was hoping to but Mrs Simkins, who was going to babysit, has gone down with some bug or another, but I'm sure you won't miss me,' Mike said this as he sat down next to Rachel in the two seater couch.

Rachel was suddenly aware of his nearness. 'In your dreams,' she said lightly. 'Miss you, of course not.' Mike looked at her intensely for a heartbeat, then grinned. 'No, too much to hope for, just take care as I won't be back until the day after tomorrow. Don't suppose you would consider staying on in town until I get back?'

Rachel shook her head. 'Sorry, Mike, but the longer I leave it the harder it will be?'

He patted her arm, 'I understand mate, don't worry. Hopefully, I will come out as soon as I get back, so two days' time, okay?'

Just then, the children came flying out of the door and Rachel knowing it was going to be hard saying goodbye got to her feet. 'I'm off now kids, be good.'

Ben launched himself at her while Em turned to her father and said, 'The lady in the library said she thought Rachel was our granny, can she be a special granny?'

Both Rachel and Mike were dumbstruck. Mike because he didn't think of Rachel as being any older than himself and Rachel who was horror-struck to have this surface again. She had been unaware that the children had taken any notice.

Mike recovered first. 'No, you have two grannies that is enough. Rachel can be an honorary aunt instead.'

'What's that?' Ben wanted to know, then the two children set up an argument as Em tried to tell him what she thought it meant and Ben didn't want to listen.

By the time they had calmed down, Rachel had regained her equilibrium and a tearful goodbye was said though Rachel tried not to let the children see her distress. As she finally drove away, the tears were trickling down her cheeks.

CHAPTER 20

The trivia night was being held at the School of Arts, which was next door to the pub. The C.W.A. ladies had organised food of which, as always, there was an abundance. Rachel was sitting with Jane and Bob, Gemma the hairdresser and finally Steve, Gemma's husband. He worked away and only came home every two weeks. But it was two weeks on and two weeks off, so it worked well. He worked at the mines. No one seemed sure exactly what he did, but he was a nice man and though he wasn't really a local he was accepted as one. Steve and Gemma had only been married for eighteen months so they were younger than the other three. They were one place short on their table, but it didn't worry them; it was all good fun.

Some questions they were all okay at, but some they were defeated. Then Jane, Rachel and Gemma all got the giggles, which rendered them incapable of saying anything sensible. The two men were beginning to get frustrated. All three girls had shared two bottles of wine, which was part of the trouble. Rachel had decided to let her hair down, especially after being mistaken for a granny!

A few onlookers had come in from the pub to see what was going on and one of them wandered over to their table. He wasn't very tall but strongly built; he had dark unruly hair and was exceedingly handsome. Everybody stared as he came in, no one had seen him before and his looks were so arresting he drew stares wherever he went, he was used to it.

As their table was near the door it was by them he stopped and just as they were debating an answer to a question, he said in a stage whisper that he knew the answer. Steve pulled out the empty chair between himself and Rachel. 'Sit down and join us, mate, we're one short as it is.'

The man sat down and quick introductions were made. His name was Patrick but everyone called him Pat he said in a soft Irish burr. He had piercing blue eyes and Rachel found them regarding her inquisitively...she realised with a jolt he was the man she had seen in the street earlier. As they broke to get refreshments he said, 'How come a beautiful woman such as yourself is here alone then?'

Rachel who had been feeling light-headed sobered up suddenly. 'My husband died,' she said baldly.

'Oh, be Jesus, I'm sorry so I am. How bad I feel asking like that.' He did look mortified.

He looked so upset Rachel felt bad then. 'It was a while ago now, what are you doing in this out of the way place, are you looking for work?'

Pat laid his finger along his nose. 'Not exactly just looking for inspiration, I'm an artist.'

'Oh.' Rachel wasn't sure she had met a real-life artist like him before. Not professional ones anyway, which she guessed he had to be.

'What sort of things do you do? Do you paint, are you a sculptor?'

'I paint a bit and this and that, I get by, so here I am exploring this neck of the woods and what should I find but a beautiful widow.'

Normally, Rachel would have given such a blatant remark the brush off, but he had such an engaging smile and a humorous twinkle in his bright blue eyes that instead of making an acid reply she grinned back at him.

'Flattery will get you nowhere, but you are welcome to stay at this table if you wish and you'll be even more welcome if you know the answers to the questions.'

Patrick smiled. 'How could a man refuse to sit here with all of you, especially one such as yourself.' And he gave a little bow of his head towards Rachel.

The rest of the evening passed in a blur for Rachel. Patrick did indeed know many answers and having trailed rather before, they now found themselves in second place at the end of the evening.

As they were all leaving, Patrick sidled up to Rachel 'May I walk you home, or are you driving? A beautiful girl such as yourself shouldn't walk home alone.'

Rachel laughed out loud at this. 'It's only about 30 yards down the road. I'm staying with Jane and Bob.'

Patrick looked disappointed but said, 'Ah, well, it was worth a try. I'll see you tomorrow so I will.'

Walking home with Jane and Bob a few minutes later, Jane remarked how Patrick had seemed interested in Rachel, who laughed. 'I was the only female there without a partner at least unless you count those young girls up the corner. Anyway, I rather think Patrick has kissed the blarney stone not once but twice at least.'

Jane nodded. 'I think you are right, but I have a feeling he'll hang around for a while, I don't think we've seen the last of him.'

CHAPTER 21

Sure enough when Rachel emerged from Jane's the next morning, there was Patrick leaning against the veranda of the pub waiting for her.

'There you are, and where might you be off to this beautiful sunny morning?'

'I'm off to the hairdressers, not that it's anything to do with you.'

'Ah, maybe not, me darlin', but I was hoping for a quiet word, I was.'

Rachel stopped, last night she had found Patrick attentions amusing but not this morning.

'Look I don't mean to be rude, but I have nothing to say to you. I am off home later and there is nothing that I can imagine that you need to have a quiet word about.'

'Well, that's where you are wrong, I told you I am an artist and I am told you have a property west of here in some really beautiful countryside. I'd like your permission to come out and do a little painting, what do you say?'

Rachel looked at her watch. 'I'm going to be late. I'll think about it while I'm in having my hair cut, OKAY?' With that, she marched off. Patrick watched her with an amused expression on his face. He was fairly certain she would agree. He had made enquiries about her in the pub after the evening had wrapped up in the hall and knew quite a lot about her.

At the hairdressers, Rachel told Gemma she wanted her hair cut, it was shoulder length normally, but she had let it go more lately so it was now halfway down her back.

'Why don't I cut it into a bob so it's just long enough to tie back but mostly you can wear it loose. Also, why don't I put a few highlights in it, you've got a few sun streaks anyway and a few grey hairs, it would look stunning, what do you say?'

Rachel smiled in the mirror at Gemma. 'Do your damnedest!'

Two hours later, Rachel emerged from the hairdressers feeling very different. With a light step, she walked across the road to the one and only clothes shop. Two pairs of shorts, one pair of jeans and two new smart tops later, she made her way to the bakery to collect her things and to be on her way.

Jane gasped when she saw her friend. 'Wow, Rach, you look amazing, I love your hair like that, it's fab.'

Rachel did a small hop and skip. 'I feel good, pity I have to get back but get back I must.'

She had also stocked up on a few essentials, and now she bought bread and a pie for her dinner. She had said goodbye to Jane and was getting into her car when a rather breathless Patrick appeared at her side.

'Oh, be Jesus, I nearly missed you, what do you say?'

Rachel had forgotten all about Patrick and his request in all the excitement of her new persona. She looked at him, he seemed harmless enough and she didn't have to see him if she didn't want to. The place was big enough.

'Okay, if you are happy to camp out, driving backwards and forwards is possible too, though I expect that would take up a lot of your time. Don't expect me to feed or entertain you, though I'm too busy for that.'

'Ah, you're a grand woman so you are, I'll follow on shortly then. I know where to come. By the way, you look more beautiful than ever, so you do.'

'Flattery will get you nowhere at all,' Rachel said for the second time and with that put the car in gear and drove off leaving Patrick watching her go with a huge grin on his face.

Two and a half hours later, Rachel, having put her shopping away and also taken a tour of the house and yards near the house, heard a motorbike. Her blood ran cold. Not Johnny or one of his sidekicks. Mike had promised her he would sort something out, but of course, there hadn't been time. She started back towards the house thinking she would get Sam's gun when the bike appeared over the rise and came towards her. It didn't look like Johnny or indeed any of his friends' bikes. It was a big bike, but it had a sidecar attached and the rider had a bright orange helmet and a blue jacket, not the normal black that Johnny and his mates wore.

Rachel stopped and waited and by the time the bike came to a stop beside her, she had guessed who it was after all she had seen him on a bike before, she remembered.

Patrick took his helmet off. 'Aw, woman, what a sight for sore eyes, both you and this place, an artist's dream.'

'I'm glad you like it, come I'll show you where you can camp or you can use the men's quarters if you like. There is no one here at present so you'll have the place to yourself and so long as you keep it clean and tidy you can do as you like. There's electricity and running water and a stove for cooking. Just don't use too much power as we are solar here and it may run short if you do.'

Pat, as he told Rachel for a second time to call him, seemed delighted with everything and Rachel left him to it telling him she would show him around the next morning.

It was funny she mused as she prepared her evening meal, deep down she had been dreading returning home after the last scare with Johnny and his pals but having Pat out there down in the men's quarters made her feel a lot safer; even though she didn't know him at all!

After sleeping well for her, Rachel was up bright and early. There was no sign that Pat was up and about, so she did her chores and had breakfast before making her way down to see if Pat was up and about. She knocked on the door, but there was no reply. Finally, she put her head round the door just as a voice said behind her, 'Top of the morning to you, grand day isn't it?'

Rachel visibly jumped. 'God, you made me jump.'

Pat smiled at her; he had a folding stool under one arm and canvas under the other and a satchel across his back.

'The light first thing was too good to miss. I've been just across there sketching and taking photos. Hope that was okay?'

Pat pointed across the main yards to a clump of gum trees that stood there; it was indeed a beautiful spot.

'You won't have had breakfast yet then?'

'Not yet, were you wanting to show me around now? I can make do with just a coffee.'

Rachel then felt bad. 'Come up to the house and I'll make you coffee and toast,' she said.

Pat sensed that though she had made the offer, she wasn't entirely comfortable saying it. He gave her the most charming smile he could muster. 'That's a grand offer, so it is, how could any man refuse, just give me a minute to put these away and I'll be with you.'

Ten minutes later, Pat was demolishing his third slice of toast and jam and talking about himself.

He was born and raised in Ireland and had come to Australia as an adventurous eighteen-year-old. He could ride so did a spell droving, then fell in love with the boss' s daughter. The marriage failed, Pat said they were both too young. He travelled round for a bit, found out that his drawings which he had always done were in demand, taught himself to use paints and had been travelling around painting and selling his work as he went ever since.

'You've never felt like settling down and staying in one place?' Rachel asked.

Pat's merry blue eyes sparkled. 'Now if I found the right woman, to be sure I'd settle down no trouble at all. Who knows I might be looking at her right now?'

Rachel blushed and got to her feet. She was out of practice flirting. 'Come now; let's see what you make of the scenery around here.'

For the rest of the day Rachel drove Pat around, they went back and had a sandwich for lunch then out again. When they got to the paddock where Rachel had found the man's body, Rachel instinctively turned the other way. Pat asked if they could go further to the right, as it looked prettier. Rachel said as briefly as she could that someone had died there recently, and she wasn't keen to go that way. Pat looked at her determined expression and shrugging, left it. Pat took many photographs and would spend ages just sitting looking at different scenes quietly. Rachel soon found out at these times, he liked to sit still and just take it all in. He explained later he was getting into the spirit of the place. Sitting quietly beside him, Rachel thought she understood what he meant.

When they finally returned home, Pat got out of Rachel's ute and giving her a small bow said, 'Thank you, me darlin'. It's been a great day. I have so much material here.' He patted his camera. 'It will take me some time to go through it all. I'll see you in the morning.'

Rachel smiled, she had enjoyed the day, but she was pleased it was over, she wasn't sure why, maybe she was just tired.

When after doing her jobs she got in and found a missed call from Mike, she tried calling him back but it was engaged, so she got on with getting her dinner and then sat down in the little office to go through her files yet again. She was about to get undressed and get in the shower when the phone rang. She hesitated, as since Johnny had come back into her life the phone ringing made her fearful, especially as it got later. Mike maybe, she thought, so with her heart racing she picked it up.

'Hello?'

'Hi, Rachel, you OKAY? Just to let you know something has come up and I can't make it out to you for a few days. Will you be okay? If you are worried come back to town, I'm sorry.'

Not having a chance to speak Rachel just said it was okay, when Mike said 'good, good, see ya' and was gone. '*Typical Mike*,' Rachel thought wryly as she got into the shower. She guessed, however, that he could pick up from her if she was worried or scared; he had before. However, she was just drying herself when the phone rang again.

She let it ring; she had an answer phone but had switched that off a few weeks ago. Finally, as it kept on and on she answered it. 'Rachel, you had me worried there.' Mike's voice sounded worried.

'Sorry, Mike, I wasn't expecting you to ring again.'

'I've just heard you have some stray Irishman staying out there, are you sure that's wise, what do you know about him, is he trustworthy?'

Rachel laughed; she couldn't help it. 'Mike it's fine he's harmless, an artist no less.'

'Humph, what sort of things does he paint, life or um... landscapes or what?'

Rachel laughed again, she couldn't help it, was Mike feeling proprietorial she wondered, did he think she would pose for Pat? 'Landscapes, scenery, maybe some cattle, nothing personal.'

'Okay, well, you take care and watch him. I'll be out soon,' with that Mike hung up. Rachel was used to his abruptness on the telephone and just smiled to herself as she got into bed.

CHAPTER 22

The next few days passed by peacefully for Rachel. Pat would arrive at the door about 9 am, and she would provide morning tea while he related what he had seen and where he had been on the property. Then if she was going across the paddocks, he would go too, bringing his camera and sketchpad with him. On those occasions, he would have a quick lunch with her when they got back, then disappear and she wouldn't see him again until the next morning. Rachel was happy with that. She didn't want to get too used to him being around, as she knew it was temporary, and though she liked him, she wasn't as comfortable in his presence as she was with Mike. She tried to work out why but couldn't really come up with an answer, not one she was ready to admit to at any rate.

It was ten days before Mike finally came bowling along, a cloud of dust behind him. Pat had just finished his coffee and Rachel was putting the empty mugs in the sink. 'Ah, here's Mike. I've told you about him, he comes to help out sometimes.'

Pat sat back in his chair looking at her. He noticed the way her eyes lit up and a small smile crinkled the corners of her mouth. Mike walked in straight across the room and gave her the briefest of hugs. He had never done that before, and Rachel was taken aback. 'Hell, woman, you look good, the way you've got your hair really suits you.'

At this point, Pat thought he should make Mike aware of his presence, as he was sure Mike hadn't noticed him when he entered the room, so he gave a small cough.

Mike swung round. 'Mike, this is Pat, the artist,' Rachel said, feeling somehow wrong footed, partly by Mike's hug.

Pat stood up. 'Pleased to meet you so I am, I've heard a lot of you.' He held out his hand.

Mike took his hand and shook it meanwhile searching Pat's face as he did so. He didn't smile, but Pat wasn't aware that Mike often looked very serious. 'Likewise,' was all he said.

For a short time, the three of them stood looking at each other, all not sure what to say. Then Rachel asked after the children and Mike drew out a chair. She put more coffee on the go and sat down to hear all she could about the children. Pat cleared his throat, 'I'll be around then.'

Rachel looked up and smiled at him. 'Okay, Pat.'

Patrick left feeling rather left out, but he didn't mind, he had lots to do.

A few days after she had returned from her stay in town, Rachel had turned Johnny's old room into an office as the glorified cupboard was so cramped and trying to lay the stud lines of the cattle out was proving difficult in the small space. She wanted help to shift furniture but didn't want to ask Pat, though she had been tempted.

'How long are you here today, Mike?'

'All day if you like, as you can see, I'm off duty.'

'Do you feel like helping me shift some furniture?'

'Why not, what do you want to do?'

Getting to her feet, Rachel led Mike through to Johnny's old room explaining as she went what she had in mind. The room was sparsely furnished as it was such a long time since Johnny had lived at home. Sam and Rachel had used it more as a dumping ground the last couple of years Sam had been around and Rachel had hardly gone in there since Sam died. Now, every time she went into her little office, she remembered Nellie and it made her sad. She didn't say this to Mike, though.

'Where shall we start?' Mike stood in the doorway looking at the jumble of boxes and general detritus where things had been shoved in there out of the way.

'Let's get rid of the bed first that will make a good space to work in.' Rachel headed towards the bed, which was only a few paces from the doorway, she caught her foot and fell onto the bed. Mike who was behind her got tangled up in her feet as they shot out and nearly ended up on top of her. He caught the head of the bed and stopped himself from landing on her but found himself looking down at her. Rachel was laughing, something Mike hadn't seen her do much in the months he had known her. Before he could stop himself, he bent down further and put his lips to hers. Rachel froze then her arms came up around his neck and she kissed him back. Then she was frantically pushing him away. They sat side by side both panting slightly.

'I'm sorry, Rachel, you just looked so lovely. I... I...'

Rachel touched his hand. 'It's alright, Mike, as much my fault as yours, forget it, okay?'

Mike sensed he would only make things more difficult if he said anything more so he just nodded and together they stood and set to work on their task.

They were both quiet to start with, but gradually, they got back to their normal working together mode and though perhaps more aware of each other than normal, nothing else happened to upset their mood.

When they broke for lunch, Rachel looked across the yard, but there was no sign of Pat. Then she saw his motorbike had gone. He had gone off on it sometimes if he was going to the further paddocks. He had taken the sidecar off at these times and now it stood in the yard looking a bit forlorn. It was very hot and Mike and Rachel took their plates of salad out onto the back veranda where there was a breeze, to eat.

'What do you know about the Irishman, Rach?' Mike suddenly said. 'Do you know what his last name is? He looked vaguely familiar.'

'No, now you come to mention it, I don't. I never thought to ask, you don't think he has a record, or something do you? He seems so harmless.'

Realising he may have upset and worried Rachel, Mike shook his head vigorously. 'No, I'm sure I've not seen him before he just reminds of someone, nothing sinister at all.'

Rachel put her head on one side thinking, then shook it. 'I don't think he reminds me of anyone, maybe I'd better watch him more; though what harm he could do out here, I can't imagine. He doesn't look like a cattle duffer.'

Mike snorted with a small laugh. 'What does a cattle duffer look like then?'

Rachel grinned at him. 'I'll tell you if I see one.'

Mike looked serious. 'Rach, I don't like you being out here alone after what happened with Johnny and his mates, gang, whatever they are, why don't you come and stay in town for a bit? The time scale he gave you will be up in six weeks and we don't know what will happen then.'

'Mike, I know what you say is true and I appreciate your concern, but I can't let Johnny drive me out of my own home. Probate should be finalised next week in any case. No, I'm not coming to town and hiding.'

'You must know by now that you are important to me, Rachel, I don't want anything bad to happen to you.'

'I'm his mother after all, Mike, he won't hurt me.' But even as she said those words, Rachel knew it was a lie, if she stood in his way there was no telling what he would do.

Mike looked at her searchingly. 'Okay, I understand, I think, but please be careful at least Pat is about. I want to set up some sort of alarm system for you so I will know if Johnny and his mates are out here but it's proving difficult to set up. I thought about giving you a radio like we carry, but I can't really do that either.'

'I will be okay, Mike, don't worry.'

Mike lent over and patted her knee. 'I hope so, Rach, as I said you are important to me, don't want to miss out on coming out here with the cattle now do I?'

But as he said this Rachel picked up, he was trying to make light of his feelings, whatever they were. He couldn't really find her that desirable, could he? After all, she had been mistaken for his children's granny. She knew her new hairstyle made her look good but not that good surely? She blushed remembering their kiss earlier. It had awakened a longing in her, don't go there she reminded herself. She looked up to see Mike regarding her and as if he read her thoughts he said lightly, 'Sorry, if I took advantage earlier, but that was some kiss!'

Rachel blushed even more and jumping to her feet grabbed Mike's plate and fled into the kitchen.

Mike followed her through but carried on into the bedroom and before long, they got back to their task. The day was just about over when at last they had Rachel's new office in some sort of order. 'I reckon I can manage now, do you want to stop to eat before you go?'

'Thanks, but I have to get back, duty calls I'm afraid. I think I heard your artist man come back a short while ago so at least you're not entirely alone.'

'Okay, thank you for everything.' Rachel had a wild desire to kiss him again but hastily stepped back. Again, Mike seemed to sense what she was thinking and with one of his rare smiles he just patted her shoulder and almost ran to his vehicle and drove away with a wave of his hand.

CHAPTER 23

The next morning, Pat later appeared for what had become a routine in the mornings. Rachel was just wondering if she should walk over and make sure he was okay when he arrived. He looked rather unwell, with rings under his eyes as if he hadn't slept and he looked pale.

'You look the worst for wear, Pat, you not well?'

Pat let out a long sigh. 'I've been better, something I've eaten I guess.'

Rachel poured him a coffee then stood looking at him as he sipped it. 'Tell you what, Pat, I'll cook you a meal tonight if you like, something to help settle your stomach.'

Pat smiled at her. 'Be Jesus, what a good woman you are to be sure.'

'I take it you'll come up then for supper?'

Pat nodded and shortly afterwards, he shuffled off still looking very sorry for himself. Rachel watched him go with a slight frown on her face; she hoped she wasn't going to have a sick man to look after.

Later, Sid turned up, as Rachel wanted both help and advice with the young bulls she had kept back. By the time they had been round finding them then looking at them and deciding what was best to do it was early afternoon. Sid departed hurriedly as he hadn't expected it to take so long. Rachel didn't mind as she had given no thought to dinner and was regretting her earlier offer.

At six o'clock, Pat arrived in the kitchen. He looked a little better having had a shave and brushed his hair down, which was often sticking up wildly. Rachel thought he needed a good haircut but was too polite to say so.

She had made a hearty soup and a new loaf of bread. She had kept it simple, not wanting to make his stomach worse. They sat silently eating for a time; Pat who was usually very eloquent was silent.

'Pat, is something else wrong, you're very quiet.'

'No, no, I'm okay thanks, just didn't sleep too well either.'

Rachel had only offered him water but now she said, 'Well, would you like a beer, or a glass of wine, there is a little left over from a party we had out here Boxing Day.'

Pat seemed to consider this for some time before he replied, 'Maybe a glass of red if that's okay? Just the one, though.'

Rachel laughed. 'You won't get much more than one. I don't think there is much left, I'll just go and see.'

However, when she got through to the pantry where she had a wine rack, she found two unopened bottles of red. Most people had been drinking beer, white or punch on Boxing Day, not red. There were a few bottles of beer too, but as they weren't in the fridge, she thought they would be rather warm. The red was too in fact, but Rachel thought she could pop an ice cube in their glasses just to cool it off a little. She supposed many people would think that was sacrilegious but who cares, she thought.

Pat's eyes lit up when she returned to the kitchen and she poured him a generous glass. 'Do you want a little ice in it to make it cooler, it's such a hot evening?'

'Oh God no, it would spoil it, just that way will be fine, thanks,' He seemed to grab the glass out of her hand.

Rachel poured herself a glass but popped some ice in it. It was a hot evening and she felt in need of something cool but now she had opened the red she thought it was a pity not to have a little.

'Here's to your painting,' she said raising her glass. Pat stopped mid sip and clinked his glass with hers.

'To be sure, here's to some painting.'

'I know you've done lots of sketches, but have you started on any actual painting yet.' Rachel was just curious.

'Jesus, woman, give me a chance, it's not something you can do in a hurry.'

'No, I suppose not, sorry.'

Pat had already finished his glass and picking up the bottle to pour himself another generous measure. *'The bottle won't last long like that,'* Rachel thought to herself.

'That was a fine soup that you made and the bread.'

'Thank you, Pat, there is some cheese, if you would like?'

He shook his head and a short time later had demolished his second glass of wine. Without a by your leave or any word at all, he finished the last of the bottle. Rachel was by now feeling uncomfortable and regretted bringing the bottle to the table. 'I think all that wine won't help settle your stomach, Pat, it will make it worse, I would think.'

'You my minder now is that it? I will judge what and how much I drink, thank you very much!' He took another loud slurp from his glass.

Rachel suddenly felt angry. It was her wine, her home, he was there because she had felt sorry for him, how dare he drink her wine then become argumentative. She stood up. 'I think you should go now before you say anything else, don't you?'

Pat got unsteadily to his feet and gave a mock bow, then stumbling slightly he made for the door. However, when he had nearly reached it, he turned back and before Rachel realised what he was doing, he picked up the other bottle from the dresser at the side where Rachel had put it and staggered out of the door. Rachel heard him swear as he almost fell down the veranda steps and she could hear him muttering to himself as he set off across the yard. She chided herself for bringing both bottles out, but at the back of her mind, she was going to put the other one in the fridge and maybe share a glass with Mike at some point.

Rachel cleared up the table, then sat down again to finish her glass of wine. She felt uneasy again now. Was Pat an alcoholic and had he done any painting? When she thought about it, she couldn't remember seeing any pictures, only sketches, which were, she supposed, good and he had taken lots of photos. Then there was the fact he had chosen to come out to her place. Other people's property was just as beautiful as hers, but it was here he had come. Had they all rejected him, or was there some other reason he was here?

All these thoughts were tumbling around in her head as after finishing her wine, she went into her new office or study as she called it to herself, and sat down to do some paperwork. She had an appointment to see her solicitor next week when probate would be finalised. She knew that wouldn't satisfy Johnny, but she hoped it would get him off her back for the time being at least. She couldn't bear the thought of selling up and at times she couldn't wait to leave. If she wasn't so frightened of Johnny and his gang maybe she would stay, as she loved the place so much. But then she was so lonely and if she had another accident like she had with her arm only worse, what then?

On impulse, she rang Mike on his mobile, but it was switched off and she wasn't game to try to get hold of him through the police station.

She had drawn the curtains after Pat's departure and after getting ready for bed and putting out the lights; she now drew them back in her bedroom and looked out at the starry night. Pat hadn't got a light burning either and the whole countryside was bathed in a silvery light from the moon which was nearly full. Rachel sighed, it looked so calm and picturesque it made her heart ache.

She got into bed but although she was tired, she couldn't sleep; the thoughts were still going round and round in her head, then just as she was drifting off the telephone went. She went through her normal ritual of not knowing whether to answer it or not, but in the end, she got out of bed and was about to speak when Mike's voice came over the phone line. 'Rachel, are you okay, what's up?' He sounded anxious.

Rachel took a deep breath; she shouldn't have phoned him. 'I'm sorry, Mike. I'm okay I didn't mean to worry you.'

'Rachel, I don't think you have ever rung me before like this, something must be up, is it Johnny?'

'No.' Rachel felt even worse now. 'I just needed to hear your voice,' she said lamely.

'Rach, come clean. Something has spooked you, I know you well enough by now, what is it?'

So, Rachel recounted Pat's behaviour then what she had been thinking about him and ended up saying she was okay but unsettled and sorry to be a pain.

'First of all, you are not a pain in any way and secondly, it sounds to me Pat has a drinking problem. Did you notice anything on trivia night?'

'No but looking back I think he was drinking juice not beer or wine, I didn't really take much notice at all.'

'Okay well, just sit tight. I don't think he'll be a threat; he has behaved until now. I'll see what I can find out and come across early in the morning, okay?'

'Thanks, Mike, I owe you.'
'Goodnight, honey, sleep well.' He was gone before Rachel could reply.

CHAPTER 24

CHAPTER 24

Rachel slept well after her conversation with Mike and woke up feeling quite refreshed, which she didn't always. She did her normal jobs then ventured down to see what Pat was up to, and if he was compos mentis or not. However, when she got there, she played it softly and called out, not too loudly. No reply.

She popped her head around the door expecting to see him asleep on the floor or something, but the room was empty, in fact though she looked everywhere, he was nowhere to be found. Having a quick look outside, Rachel took a chance and walked over to look at some of his 'paintings' he had stacked against a wall. All she could find were rough sketches, nothing very definite at all. Then on closer inspection she realised most of them were down at the creek near where the man's body had been found. Why was that? she wondered, it was odd.

She looked around at the rest of his things, which were mostly put away neatly. The second wine bottle was near the sink, there was no sign of a glass so Rachel guessed he had drunk straight from the bottle. There was a pile of papers on the table and she felt very tempted to have a quick look but decided that was snooping and refrained from doing so. She frowned and went back outside; his motorbike and sidecar were still there so he couldn't have gone far.

She was still standing considering what to do when she heard a car and looked up saw Mike, at least, she thought it was Mike, coming down the track towards her house. However, as it got closer, Rachel could see it wasn't Mike. It was a police car, yes, but Josh was driving it and he was alone.

With a feeling of dread in her stomach, Rachel walked back towards the house to meet him.

'I expected Mike, Josh, is anything wrong,' Rachel blurted out before Josh could speak.

'No, Rachel, don't worry, Mike couldn't get away this morning, there is a lot going on right now, but he was concerned about this Irish bloke and you, so he asked me to come out and check if you were okay?'

'I'm fine.' Rachel swallowed the lump of disappointment that stuck in her throat. She acknowledged to herself that she had been longing to see Mike. She was so happy around him and so safe. Was that how she felt? Was she just a lonely old woman, well not old, but lonely?

Josh stood looking at her. 'Rachel?'

'Oh sorry, Josh, I was thinking.'

'It didn't look like they were happy thoughts. How's the Irishman this morning? Mike said it sounds as if he has a drinking problem?'

So Rachel related the previous night's happenings and how Pat had made off with the second bottle of red. Together they had another look in the building and walked around outside, but as it was very dry they couldn't see where he had gone. There were no footprints to follow. Josh stayed with her for a while as she did her jobs. They both wondered briefly if he had gone in the chook pen as the gate wasn't secured properly, but there was no sign.

'Would you like a coffee or something before you head back, Josh?'

'Nah, thanks, a nice cold glass of water though if that's okay.'

A few minutes later, having assured Josh she would be okay, Rachel watched him drive away.

She decided to go back indoors as it really was stinking hot and she had plenty of paperwork to do. Sitting down in her new office, she felt so sad suddenly. Sam was dead and gone, she was very attracted to Mike, maybe she even loved him, but he was too young and married, he might find her attractive but more for a quick fling, not for anything lasting. Then there was Johnny. Why was he being so threatening? What was it he was really after? Was it just money? He seemed to hate her so much but what had she ever done to him? On top of all that was the Irishman, what was his problem and why did he have to come and be such a nuisance? It had been okay to start with but she had gotten rather fed up with him being here the last few days and now he had really blown it. She would tell him to leave when he came back, she decided.

The day dragged on, it was very hot with no clouds and the sun was beating down relentlessly. Rachel had a quick break; she had made some progress sorting out the stud papers. When Sam was ill and then since he had died, she had only done what was essential, and some papers were in rather a muddle and needed to be brought up to date. Having immersed herself in her task, she felt better and managed to put her sad thoughts to one side. Going back into the office, she wondered if Patrick was back but thought she would check on him later. She worked steadily and at five o'clock, she got up, stretched and thought she would just go see if Patrick was okay... She still felt angry but also a little responsible so checking on him was the least she could do. She certainly wasn't about to invite him back to the house in a hurry.

When she got down to the men's quarters though Patrick wasn't there, everything looked just as it had that morning and a small seed of disquiet settled onto Rachel. Where could he be? She walked in a large circle around the immediate part of the property looking into other buildings and places where he might be. She was now getting more and more concerned. The sun and heat had been relentless and if he had wandered off drunk the night before and maybe fallen and hurt himself, he might be in enormous trouble by now.

Going back to her house, she let the dogs off and called to them got into the ute and set off across the paddocks, not really knowing which way to go. However, the light was fading fast now and before long, she turned back; it was useless to drive aimlessly around like this. Maybe she had missed something. But of course, nothing had changed when she got back, and by now she was really worried. She tied the dogs up again and fed them and shut up the chooks, all the time wondering what the best thing was to do.

Finally, when she got to the house, she decided to ring Mike and talk to him. Part of her thought it was up to Patrick what he did, or where he went, but the other part of her was worried that something awful had happened.

She rang the police station and got Josh, with some embarrassment she asked to speak to Mike. 'He isn't here right now, Rachel, can I help?'

'It's just that Patrick hasn't turned up yet and I don't quite know what to do. It's been so hot today and if he hasn't got at least water with him, well...' she trailed off.

'I see, wait a minute, I think Mike has just returned, I'll put him on.'

'Hi, Rachel, I'm sorry today has been one of those days I'm afraid. I gather the Irishman is still hiding or whatever he's playing at?'

'Yes, he hasn't come back, and it's been so hot today and as far as I can tell he hasn't got any water or anything with him. I feel responsible since it was my fault, he got the wine and got drunk.'

'TSK, Rachel, of course it's not your fault, he's a grown up, not a youngster. It's dark now and I don't think there is much good driving around in the dark. Sit tight I'll come out in the morning first light and we'll find him. Okay? Take care, mate.' Mike hung up.

Rachel stood looking at the phone, then sighed. Mike was always so odd on the phone, so brief, she wished he had at least talked to her more. She sighed and putting the phone down went into the kitchen to get herself some supper. She had to force herself to eat as she was again too wound up. '*This is getting silly,*' she thought. '*I always seem to be worrying about something or someone.*'

Every little while, she looked out of the window hoping to see lights come on down in the men's quarters, but nothing happened. When finally, she was tired enough to go to bed, she got her torch and getting Sam's gun she made her way down. But everything was the same as it had been that morning, and reluctantly she went back to the house and got into bed.

CHAPTER 25

Rachel jerked awake, a car! She looked at the clock it was 4.30 am and would be getting light soon; it must be Mike.

She climbed out of bed and dressed quickly. She could just make out the police vehicle that Mike drove when he was on duty. She went down the veranda steps and tapped on the driver's window. Mike had been engrossed in his tablet, which he had on his lap. He jumped!

Winding down the window he said, 'God, woman, you gave me a fright.'

Rachel grinned back at him, she felt ridiculously pleased to see him. 'Want a cuppa before we start?'

'Sounds good, I didn't mean to disturb you, but yes, a good strong coffee would be great, thanks.'

Looking at him in the light of the kitchen, Rachel thought he looked very tired and worried too. She had never seen him look like that before; she put her hand on his arm. 'Are you okay, Mike, you look really tired.'

He patted her hand then moved his arm away. 'Yes, long spell on duty, always makes me tired; I'm fine really, thanks. I thought it would be best if it's just you and me to start with then if we can't see hide nor hair of him, we'll call in the troops. I've put Josh on alert just in case.'

Rachel was busy making the coffee; she turned and smiled at him. 'Yes, you are right, no need to panic, stupid bloke, actually I've had an idea where we should look, he has done loads of sketches of the creek where that man's body was found. Or at least near there, so perhaps that's where we should start.'

Mike sat looking at her for several seconds before saying, 'Perhaps there's a connection, the guy we found was an Irishman called Shawn O'Leary, it took us sometime to find that out and I don't think I ever mentioned his name to you?'

Rachel shook her head. 'I've never asked Pat his surname, but even if I had he may not have told me the truth. I must admit I have been wondering why he chose to come here as there are plenty of other beautiful places around, Sid's next door for example.'

'I just thought he was after you,' Mike said.

Rachel laughed, not taking him seriously, but the laughter died when she saw Mike's expression, he looked serious and almost angry. 'Don't be silly, why would he be interested in me?' She didn't mean it to come out as a question, more a statement but Mike's gaze intensified.

'Why wouldn't he be, you mean, you are a very desirable woman.'

For a moment, the atmosphere in the kitchen seemed charged with emotion, but neither of them wanted to make a move and Mike suddenly got to his feet. 'Come on, we've an Irish leprechaun to find.'

Feeling rather shaken by their exchange, Rachel followed him out to the police SUV and they set off.

'We must be systematic in this search, so I suggest we start at the furthest paddock where we found O'Leary, search that one and work our way back here. If that fails, we will have to call in help. S.E.S. and locals, but I think he's big enough and ugly enough, anyway.'

Rachel smiled to herself, she couldn't help it, was Mike showing signs of jealousy? Surely not!

When they got to the paddock in question, Rachel felt an irrational dread creep into her body. She felt nervous and very apprehensive. However, she didn't want Mike to see how she was affected so she jumped out and opened the gate, shutting it after he had driven through. As she climbed back into the car, Mike looked at her and said, 'Are you good to go, or do you want to wait here?'

Rachel shook her head. 'It's fine, Mike, I just haven't been to that part of the paddock since I found that man, but it will be fine I'm sure.'

As they crested the small rise and started down towards the creek, Rachel found she was holding her breath. There was no one there and no sign that they could see. They drove as far along the creek as they could, then started back the other way. 'When we get to the shallow place, we'll drive across as far as Sid's boundary.'

'Let's go to the swimming hole first before we cross over,' Rachel said. 'There is more shelter there if he got this far, it would have taken him a couple of hours or so to get to this paddock and he would have been pretty thirsty by then. I showed him the place to swim when I showed him round.'

As they approached, they could see a man propped up against one of the tall gums that grew in a cluster near the creek.

As Mike pulled up, the man struggled to his feet, but he looked as if he felt very unwell and sat down again with a thump. Rachel got out of the car, but she didn't hurry even though Patrick looked bad. She still felt rather angry and there was an element of distrust there.

When she got to him though, she couldn't help feeling a little sorry for him. He looked as if he had fallen over a few times by how grubby he was. He was wearing the same clothes he had on when he had come to dinner and there was a big tear in his jeans. He hadn't got a hat on and his face looked red and sore, his lips were cracked, his hair was all tangled and he had a growth of gingery beard around his face. Suddenly, Rachel could see the resemblance to the man she had found dead. 'You look a sorry sight, whatever possessed you to go off like that? You could have died out here you know.'

Patrick struggled to his feet again. 'Be Jesus, woman, I know. I'm sorry, it's just...it's just.' His voice was a hoarse whisper.

Mike intervened, 'Was Shawn O'Leary your relative by any chance?'

Pat nodded dumbly, then said in his whispery voice, 'He said he'd found gold, I've been looking and looking but if he's hidden it, I can't find it.'

Rachel handed him the water bottle she had brought, 'Just sip it, Pat, don't gulp it,' she warned.

He did as he was told and after a bit, he started to look a little better. Rachel guessed that his main trouble dehydration. Mike stood by, watching with a grim expression on his face.

'Right, now we will go back, and I need to talk to you, Patrick.' Mike sounded very brusque and businesslike. Pat looked as if he would put up an argument but having seen the expression on Mike's face decided against it.

By the time they got back, he was looking much better, having sipped water nearly the whole way. Mike led the way into the quarters where Pat's things were and said, 'Sit down, Patrick; I want the truth now, all of it.'

'Where shall I start? When I came here or—'

Mike cut him off. 'Start by telling us your relationship to Shawn.'

Pat sat looking at his hands for a minute then pulling himself together began to speak, 'We're brothers; at least we were until the silly bugger died.' Rachel saw tears glistening in Pat's eyes as he stopped again.

'Go on,' she said gently.

'He was quite a bit older than me, but I suppose we were close; at least I worshipped him as my big brother and followed him about everywhere. My Pa and Shawn fought like mad though, and Pa liked his grog, and when he'd had a bit to drink, we all kept out of his way. I don't really know what happened, but they had a big bust up and the next day Shawn had gone. We none of us knew where. My mother was beside herself, but he was gone and that seemed to be that. I got on okay at school and when I left, I trained to be a draughtsman. My other brothers and sisters weren't worried anymore about Shawn, he was the eldest and I guess none of them were close to him except for me. I got the chance of a job out here. I got bored after a while though and well you know how I bummed around. Then one day there was Shawn. I couldn't believe my luck, there he was. He looked bad to my eyes though, and I guessed the grog had got him. He was travelling around getting work where he could, much the same as me really. We travelled together for a time then I realised I liked the drink too much too; I couldn't stop. I couldn't paint, which was what I was doing by then, I couldn't function properly at all. So, I stopped drinking, I laid off, but Shawn was too far-gone I reckon, at least he didn't really want to stop. We parted company again but kept in touch. Infrequently, I admit but in touch, nevertheless.

'About six months ago, Shawn rang me on the mobile, first time he had ever done that, so I knew it was important. Said he had found gold but some gang or another was after him, said he would hide it and get it at a later date. I asked him where he was, but he didn't want to tell me, said it was safer for me not to know, I didn't hear from him again. Then the police down in Roma got in touch a few months ago, they were looking for people with the same surname, I was near Darwin, took me a while to get here. Well, you know the rest.' At this point, Pat let the tears run down his cheeks; he brushed them away angrily. 'He might have made it up as when he'd had a bit to drink, he'd make up stories, but get confused between fact and fiction sometimes.'

Mike and Rachel had listened in silence. Now Rachel burst out, 'Why didn't you tell me? Why all the deceit?'

'I'm sorry, Rachel, I didn't want to draw you into anything and I'm not sure what the truth is.'

Rachel felt angry and sorry for Patrick all at the same time. She turned away; she'd make a drink, then leave. She made Patrick an instant coffee while Mike questioned Pat further, then excusing herself, walked back to the house. She felt exhausted all of a sudden and depressed. She threw herself down on the veranda sofa and closed her eyes.

CHAPTER 26

Rachel jumped and looked around, not knowing where she was for a second, then she saw Mike sitting on the other chair watching her. He had a strange expression on his face but all he said was, 'Sorry to wake you, darlin', but I must go.'

'I'm sorry I must have dropped off.'

'You look as if you need sleep, Rach, I don't think you sleep very well, do you?'

Rachel shook her head, not wanting to tell a lie but not wanting to tell the truth either. 'How's Pat?'

Mike frowned. 'Okay, it's a pity we, or rather I, didn't make a connection earlier. Shawn had hidden his personal documents in his ute, not that well, since he'd taped them underneath the passenger seat. The guys down in Roma found them; it was all taken there after it was found.' Rachel nodded, she remembered. 'He was one scared bloke it seems. Pat said when he'd had a skin full, he would see aliens coming out of the bush to get him, all sorts of weird things. I don't know whether to believe Pat or not, neither do I know what to think about hidden gold.'

Rachel stood up and stretched. 'It all sounds rather far-fetched to me, time for a cuppa?'

Mike shook his head. 'Sorry, I must dash, catch you later.' He gave her shoulder a quick squeeze as he walked by her, then down the steps and moments later, he was speeding away.

Having watched him go with a heavy heart, Rachel went indoors and made a drink, then remembered that she hadn't done any of her normal morning chores. The chooks were very pleased to see her and their antics when she let them out, cheered her up no end. There was no sign of Pat, and she didn't feel like seeing him. Going back indoors, she decided to ring

Norma and have a chat. They didn't do this often, even less lately, but Rachel always knew that Norma was more than happy to have a catch up.

It wasn't far into the conversation before she was telling Norma about Patrick and his brother. Norma was quiet for a few moments then said, 'I remember that Allen said he seemed very jumpy and asked where the old homestead was. He was pretty drunk too. Allen told him the boss was away and to get lost, I think he felt bad about it when the guy was found dead.'

'Pat says his brother was often imagining things when he was drunk. I think he used to hallucinate from time to time so who knows,' Rachel said.

They chatted on for a time then said their goodbyes, Norma telling Rachel to come over soon and have dinner. It was something she and Sam used to do from time to time, but since Sam's death Rachel had been reluctant to go and Norm, sensitive to Rachel's feelings, hadn't asked her for a long time.

Rachel went across to the big paddock where the cows and calves were. She had two bulls and one of them was in that paddock while the other would be put in with the cows soon. She looked for and found her special calf that Mike had helped birth. She found her near her mother; she was growing fast. The little animal saw Rachel and came running up to her for a scratch, Rachel acknowledged to herself she had spoiled her. 'We'll have to name you, won't we?' she said, stroking her long velvety ears. 'I think 'Maisie', what do you think?'

Maisie just leaned into Rachel, she was enjoying the funny things this human did, she was very good at scratching places Maisie couldn't reach herself.

The warmth of the little animal and the enjoyment of their exchange suddenly made Rachel feel sad. Here she was alone with only a calf to love her, now Nellie was gone. Pity Mike was so far from her reach because she...loved him?

This thought came unbidden into her mind and she drew her breath in sharply. Slowly she came to terms with this knowledge, yes, she did, she loved him. In some ways, he was not unlike Sam, calm, quiet and kind, but in other ways so different. She mentally shook herself; Mike was attracted to her she knew, but it was a physical thing, she was sure not love, not really. He was married and younger, he might like a brief affair but nothing long term. She was too old. This thought depressed her again and giving Maisie one last pat, she hurried back to the house.

Looking out of the kitchen window later as darkness fell, she saw Pat had put a light on and decided there and then to go down and see him. She didn't want him around anymore. He would have to go and now was as good a time as any to tell him.

He was sitting at the table when she tapped on the door and walked in. He had put on clean clothes and shaved. He still looked rather peaky, but much better than he had even before she had invited him to dinner.

'Rachel, my lovely, how sorry I am that I've caused you so much stress. It was never my intention. Can you forgive me?'

He was so good looking and looking at her with his blue eyes pleading and a winning smile on his face, Rachel felt her resolve weakening.

'I'm not happy, Pat, why didn't you just tell me you were Shawn's brother. I didn't know his name, but I would have been sympathetic.'

Pat got to his feet and came and stood in front of her. 'Ahh, Jesus, woman, you are so beautiful when you are cross, so you are.' Bending forward swiftly he kissed her on the lips.

Rachel recoiled. 'What do you think you're doing?'

Pat just grinned at her. 'Just thanking a beautiful woman for her kindness and understanding. I'm guessing that you might get lonely sometimes as I do, perhaps we could be company for each other. Now you know my little secret, to be sure we could have some fun together.'

Rachel knew she should be angry and send him packing especially now he was coming onto her but standing in front of her with a big grin on his handsome face, she couldn't find any anger so she merely said, 'In your dreams, O'Leary, behave or else you'll have your marching orders.' With that, she left and returned to the house. She was aware he was watching her all the way, though.

CHAPTER 27

For the next few days, Rachel kept out of Patrick's way as much as she could, which really was quite easy. He didn't come up to the house as he had been doing, he seemed to be keeping a low profile too. Rachel was grateful for that, but her emotions seemed to be jumping around all over the place. She hadn't heard any more from Johnny or his cronies, she was anxious about that. She had been granted probate and put some money aside to buy Johnny off, though she couldn't see that happening. Her quick trip to see the solicitor had worried her more than set her mind at rest and now she found she had no end of paper-work to plough through.

Now that she had come to terms with the fact that she loved Mike, but he was out of reach, it had made her feel very depressed. She still missed Sam and still loved him too or at least, she told herself, his memory. He had told her before he died to find someone else if she could, so she didn't feel disloyal, as she might have done, just that she had picked the wrong man.

As for Patrick and his troubles, she put them to the back of her mind, if he did nothing else to bother her, he could stay. It made her feel safer with him being around anyway.

Mike was still ringing her at least once a day, but the calls were very brief even by Mike's standards, he was very busy he said. He did emphasise, though; she was to let him know if Pat was any more of a problem. 'I've hardly seen him,' Rachel replied.

'Good, if he goes off again just let him go, he isn't your responsibility, Okay?'

Rachel agreed, she didn't want to worry about that too. The time scale that Johnny had given her was getting closer and closer, and she was getting more and more stressed.

It was a scorching day, too hot almost to think straight. She hadn't seen Mike for a couple of weeks now, not since Pat's disappearance, feeling restless and seeing Pat's bike was there, Rachel decided to walk down and see him. She had seen him briefly as she kept him supplied with eggs and veggies out of her garden, but they had been very brief meetings and Pat had seemed silent and a bit out of sorts.

She knocked on the door and heard a muffled 'come in'. Walking in, she couldn't see Pat to start with, then he emerged from the shower. He only had a towel round his body, his hair was still wet and hung in loose curls down his head. He was strongly built and the words 'Greek God' flitted through Rachel's mind. He was very pleasing to look at. Feeling very flustered now, Rachel stuttered that she thought she would just come and see if he was okay.

'Sure, I'm okay, how's yourself, here take a seat.' Pat didn't seem at all put out that she had caught him nearly naked. Feeling uncomfortable, Rachel perched on the edge of the chair by the table.

Patrick offered her tea, but she shook her head and searched around for something to say. She couldn't help noticing his muscular physique and was very aware of his masculinity. Pat stood looking at her then said, 'Oh, be Jesus, I wish I could paint you, would you let me?'

Rachel stared at him. 'A portrait you mean?'

'No, woman, not a portrait, a life drawing you have a gorgeous figure, fine bone structure, when you move you are so graceful and I bet under those clothes you are even more lovely. Those long brown legs, they nearly drive a man wild!' Patrick hadn't sat down and now Rachel was aware that he had a rather obvious erection. She leapt to her feet, angry and alarmed.

'Don't come near me!'

Pat took a couple of steps back and put his hands palm up in a placating gesture.

'Sorry, so I am, I meant what I said but I wouldn't do anything to hurt or upset you, I had to try, you are one lovely woman so you are. Forgive me?'

He looked at her so pleadingly that once again Rachel relented.

'Okay, just put some clothes on and I will have a cup of tea, thanks.'

Pat gave a mock bow and went off to get dressed, though when he came back, he only had a pair of very short shorts on which, in Rachel's view, was just as bad as the towel.

However, he set about making tea then sat down at the table companionably. Before long, they were chatting away. Then Rachel asked him about his brother. 'Do you really think he'd got some gold from somewhere or that it was just a dream?' she asked.

'I honestly don't know, he said he was exploring some wild gorge country near Alice in the Northern Territory and found this nugget just lying there. He picked it up and high tailed it out. He didn't tell me much more but when he'd had a bit to drink, his judgement could be way off, so maybe he's told someone else, who knows.'

Rachel sat thinking then she said, 'You said something about someone was after him?'

Pat shook his head slightly. 'The last time I spoke to him, he was on his way in this direction from near the Isa, so he said. He kept saying someone wanted to steal his gold, though I think he said 'they', he was very garbled, and I had a job to make sense of what he was saying.'

Rachel sat looking at Pat, he was very upset she could see. She laid her hand on his arm. 'When did you hear he had died?'

'I was actually in the Northern Territory when the Roma police phoned me; they found my number among Shawn's things, silly bugger why didn't he just come to meet me?' Now the tears ran down Patrick's cheeks.

Rachel stroked his arm. 'He wasn't a very well man, was he Pat? It could have happened any time.'

'I know so I do but to die out here and alone, it just seems so, so unfair!'

They sat in silence for a time, Rachel was still stroking Pat's arm though wasn't aware of it, she was thinking about the two brothers and how sad that Shawn had drunk himself to death. She looked up to find Pat's eyes fixed on her; they were so blue, they looked like sapphires. Pat leaned towards her and kissed her gently on the lips. 'You're a lovely woman so you are, are you sure you don't want to have a little cuddle?'

Rachel laughed she couldn't help it. 'I'll give you full marks for trying, Patrick O'Leary, but no, you're a nice man but no thank you.'

Pat smiled at her wistfully. 'Does that fella Mike know how lucky he is?'

Rachel blushed and felt very hot. 'I don't know what you mean,' she got to her feet as she said this, feeling very embarrassed.

'To be sure, I've seen the way you look at each other, any fool can see that. Don't waste time, life is too short.'

'If you think that, why did you try it on with me?' Rachel was trying to get away from her own feelings, but, she wanted to know why Pat had tried to get her into bed with him.

'Because you are a very attractive woman and I'm guessing Mike hasn't made a play; so, I thought I would, why not? I kinda knew it wouldn't work, but I had to try, I have trouble sleeping some nights because of you!'

'Oh.' Rachel was now completely nonplussed as to what to say. Again, there was silence for a time, then clearing her throat, Rachel moved towards the door. Then stepping back towards him, she bent down and kissed Pat briefly on the cheek. 'Thanks, Pat, see you tomorrow.' And with that she returned to the house.

CHAPTER 28

At 2am Rachel woke, her heart hammering in her chest. A motorbike coming nearer then – it was going away. She lay still, listening; it was Patrick she thought, what was he up to now? Getting out of bed, she peered out of the window looking toward the men's quarters but it was a very dark night. The only thing she was sure of was that there were no lights. Feeling her way, she crept through to the front of the house; it would be a different view. Going out onto the veranda, she could make out the sheds and yards, but it was so dark, there was nothing to see, just the velvety sky with all the little pin pricks of light where the stars were. After standing there for a bit, she went back indoors. She knew she wouldn't get back to sleep easily, so she made a drink and sat down at the kitchen table. Her afternoon with Patrick played out again in her mind. She had shut the thoughts out when she went to bed, but now they resurfaced, and her mind was in overdrive.

Now she had admitted to herself she loved Mike; she turned her mind to how he felt. She understood he wanted to make love to her but there was this issue with their age difference, and of course, he was still married, how long for? But still married, nonetheless. Then she thought about what Pat had said to her. Should she take a chance with Mike if the opportunity arose, even if it didn't work out. Should she take whatever Mike offered her even if it was just a brief affair? She didn't know what to think or what she should do. Eventually she decided to just go with the flow, if it happened, it happened. Then her thoughts turned to Johnny, when would he show up? She had lost count of the weeks he had given her. She reckoned she had two-and-a-half weeks left before he showed up. She shuddered. '*The shit will hit the fan then,*' she thought to herself. Finally, she dragged herself off to bed, none of her worries resolved.

The next morning, she looked out to discover that both Pat's motorbike and sidecar had gone. Feeling worried, she went down to see if he had merely moved them out of sight but in her heart, she knew he'd gone. Walking into the building, her fears were confirmed. It felt empty even before she saw that all his belongings were gone. Everything was neat and tidy and clean. She would miss him; she had felt safer with him there. Also, Johnny hadn't been here while Patrick was around, was it because he knew there was someone else there? How could he though, that was silly, she chided herself.

Turning to go, she saw an envelope lying on the table with her name on it. Picking it up, she carried it with her back to the house. She made coffee and sat at the table and drew out the note. Patrick had bold italic writing; it suited his personality she thought randomly.

My dear Rachel,

I thought I would go before I overstayed my welcome. It has been great staying here, and I felt close to Shawn. We had hardly seen each other in years but his passing has left a big hole in my heart, I can't explain it. I'm sorry I came on too strongly but you are one desirable woman and I meant it when I said I wanted to paint you, if you agreed I'd even let you keep your clothes on!

I guess the gold thing was just Shawn's imagination, so I'll just forget it.

Don't waste your life, lovely woman, if Mike doesn't want you let me know, I'll happily fill his shoes.

Take care; I know you have many who love you; I found that out in town, they all watch out for you.

Your greatest admirer and frustrated lover,
Patrick O'Leary.

Rachel found she had a big lump in her throat after reading his letter. She would miss him quite a lot, his ready smile, his bright blue eyes that sometimes would sparkle with mischief, he was so good looking maybe she shouldn't have knocked him back; he was probably a good lover.

What was she thinking?! That was the last complication she needed. Getting up, she busied herself getting her morning chores done.

For a time she was taken up with all the cattle related jobs she had, and it wasn't really until darkness fell that her thoughts returned to her loneliness. The feeling came back and she realised that Pat being around had meant more to her peace of mind than she had acknowledged before. On impulse, she rang Norma and had a chat. It was something she only did very occasionally and hardly ever lately; though, it was the second time lately. Norma picked up Rachel's underlying disquiet and kept her talking as long as she could without making it too obvious to Rachel, she knew she was uncomfortable. Rachel never wanted people to pick up on her vulnerability, and Norma was aware of this. Finally, she said, 'Rachel, you haven't been here for dinner in a very long time, why don't you come over tomorrow evening?'

Rachel didn't know what to say, as it would mean driving back after dark, could she do that she asked herself. At length, she thanked Norma and was about to refuse when she heard herself saying she'd love to.

She put the phone down, thinking what an idiot, but also looking forward to going. She made herself some soup, but every little noise had her listening with her heart thumping, her head was telling her to stop being so silly but she couldn't seem to help it. At ten o'clock, she thought she would have a shower and maybe sleep in the chair again. She hadn't done that since Pat had been there, then the phone rang. thinking it was Mike she answered it quickly. There was silence on the other end, no not silence she could hear someone breathing. Really spooked, she slammed the phone down. She had only answered it, she hadn't made a big thing when the person didn't speak, maybe it was just a wrong number. She didn't really believe that, though. Then it rang again. She would let it ring out, but in the end, she snatched it up. 'What do you want?' she almost screamed into the receiver.

'Rach, what's up?'

'Mike! Oh, Mike,' Rachel started to cry, she couldn't stop herself.

'Rachel, has Johnny come, is that it, what is it, Rachel?'

Taking a deep breath, Rachel managed to tell Mike about the phone call a moment or two before, then she told him that Patrick had gone.

Mike was quiet, so quiet that Rachel thought he'd hung up or something and was about to speak when he said, 'Hang in there, I'll come over.' The phone then went click before she said anything else.

She stood staring at the phone in her hand, she knew Mike had a lot on, she never asked about police business and he never said, it seemed like an unspoken arrangement that they had between them. But now, she felt guilty she was being a weak and needy woman. She tried his mobile, but it was switched off and she didn't feel comfortable ringing the station, so she sat at the table and waited to see if he did come. She put some coffee on, he could have a quick drink before he headed back, she thought. She remembered he had said he hadn't got any time off for two more days. He would come out and see her then, they had arranged that the other evening when he had rung her.

Time seemed to slow, and she felt tired but didn't want to get into the shower until Mike had been. Then she thought she would as it was now getting late. Maybe he wasn't coming after all. She went through into the bedroom and undressing, got quickly into the shower, she made it a quick one then remembered she had put the coffee machine on but had she put any water in it? She couldn't remember. She grabbed a towel, wrapped it around her body and rushed through to the kitchen, hoping the machine was all right. She pulled up short in the doorway, Mike was sitting at the table, he stood as she stopped. They were both standing still looking at each other, then Mike strode across the intervening space and taking her in his arms, put his lips to hers kissing her fervently. Pulling away slightly he said, 'God, woman, you look good, I'm sorry, I haven't got here sooner.'

Rachel put her finger gently across his lips, his kiss had inflamed her desire, 'ssh' putting her arms around his neck she kissed him again. Her towel slipped to the floor and Rachel attempted to stop it, but it was too late, Mike stopped her. 'Leave it, Rach, you're so lovely, allow me...' He picked her up and carried her through to the bedroom and laid her gently on the bed. Rachel lay quietly as he rapidly undressed and laid down beside her, caressing her, kissing her, stroking her. 'Those beautiful breasts of yours have haunted me ever since you broke your arm,' he whispered.

There was passion in their lovemaking, but they took it slowly, not really wanting it to end. There was a deep need within both of them and their lovemaking was passionate but not frantic as they both savoured every kiss, every caress and when they both finally reached a climax, it was very fulfilling for them both.

Afterwards, Rachel lying on her side said, 'Mike that was wonderful, so wonderful, thank you.'

Mike grinned; he looked like a cat who had swallowed the cream. 'I've never had anyone thank me before, maybe I should thank you.'

Rachel felt a bit silly then and getting up she found her dressing gown and said, 'Let's see what the coffee is doing shall we.'

Mike followed her through to the kitchen and they sat again at the table. The coffee machine, which was old and temperamental, had switched itself off again so Rachel put on the kettle for tea.

Mike took her hand in his. 'That was very special, Rach, but I'm supposed to be somewhere else, will you be okay if I go in a minute, I'm sorry but duty calls. I've been much longer than I intended. I wasn't expecting to make love to you, at least not tonight.'

'I understand, Mike, I'll be fine, I promise. I've lots to tell you, but nothing that can't wait.'

Mike stood up and going back to the bedroom hastily got dressed. Soon, he was driving away with a promise to come the day after tomorrow.

Rachel got into bed and hugging the sheet that seemed to smell slightly of their lovemaking, fell into a very deep sleep.

CHAPTER 29

When Rachel woke the next morning, she didn't hurry out of bed as she normally did but lay there remembering every kiss and caress of the night before. She felt happier than she had at any time since Sam died, and when she eventually got up, she started her chores with a smile on her face. However, during the morning the euphoria gradually dwindled as thinking about Johnny, then wondering how long Mike would be interested in her and all her other worries resurfaced. By lunch time she was nearly back to her mood from the day before.

Going indoors to get herself something to eat, she heard the phone ringing, her heart leapt. 'Mike' was her first thought but picking it up there was silence like the night before. She hung up quickly and almost at once, it rang again, she snatched it up. 'Look here you moron...' Anger took over.

'That's not a nice way to speak to your one and only, Ma, now is it?' Johnny's voice taunted her over the telephone line.

Rachel was silent to start with as she gathered her wits. 'I thought you were someone else.'

'Really? Still not a nice way to talk Ma, now is it? I just rang to see how you are getting on selling the cattle and stuff so I can take the farm over.'

'What do you want with the farm, Johnny, it's never interested you before?'

'Maybe I've changed, but in any case, it's none of your business. Times nearly up Ma, and I don't think you're moving the cattle quickly enough. Maybe you want a reminder, all sorts of things can happen to a woman out there on her own.' With that, he hung up, leaving Rachel staring at the receiver in horror.

In the event, after that phone call, Rachel spent all afternoon going round securing everything she could. She figured the dogs would be okay and she couldn't do much about the cattle. She put her old horse in the round yard close to the house. She found some old padlocks and used them to lock the men's quarters and various other things she thought of. Then she worried about going to Sid and Norma's that evening for dinner. Taking the bull by the horns, she rang Norma.

'Norma, I'm really sorry but I don't think I will make it tonight, something has happened, and I don't think I can leave.'

Norma was so quiet for so long Rachel thought they had been cut off. 'Norma?'

'Sorry, Rach, I'm here, look I don't want to pry but has this something to do with Johnny?'

'Yea, I didn't want to tell you, but yep, Johnny.'

'Can we do something, Rach, what's he done? Come on love, you can't fight this on your own, come on, what is it?'

Rachel burst into tears and slowly she told Norma the whole sorry story, right from the night he put in an appearance until that day. Norma was quiet for a time then she said, 'My God, Rachel, we had no idea things were this bad, why didn't you tell us? Does Mike know any of this?'

Rachel gulped and tried to regain control. 'Yes, he doesn't know about today, but he knows everything else.'

Norma tut-tutted. 'Well, I think he should do more, whatever is it coming to for God's sake? I've a good mind to ring him and give him a piece of my mind!'

Rachel felt quite alarmed by this; whatever would Norma think if she knew about last night, in the event Mike and she hadn't done much talking.

'No, please don't do that, I trust Mike and I'm sure he's doing all he can. He phones me every day.'

Norma huffed but seemed to accept what Rachel said. They finished their conversation without resolving anything. Rachel was aware that both Norma and Sid thought Mike should have done more on Boxing Day and a little niggling doubt made her wonder about that too, but she shut those thoughts out. Mike wasn't a coward, he had her best interests at heart she was sure, wasn't she?

Feeling restless, scared, generally out of sorts, she collected Sam's gun and took it with her to shut the chooks up. It was just on dusk and she felt very fearful and couldn't get back to the house quick enough. She then went round making the house as secure as she possibly could.

A little later she was standing in the kitchen wondering what to get for her supper when the phone went. She had to force herself to answer it but it seemed unlikely it was Johnny. It wasn't, it was Mike. 'Hi, honey, how's things? Are you okay?'

'No, Johnny rang. I'm scared, Mike.'

'Did he threaten you? What did he say?'

'He said time was nearly up and all sort of things could happen to a woman on her own.'

'MMmmm. I don't like the sound of that either, given what has happened so far. Look Rachel, I really think you should come into town and stay with Jane for the time being anyway.'

Just then, Rachel heard a vehicle outside. 'Mike, someone has just come!'

'Okay, don't panic, peep out and see who it is but stay on the phone.'

Rachel edged towards the window and looked out, then laughed with relief as she could see Sid in the headlights and Norma just getting out of the car from the passenger side.

'It's okay, Mike, it's Norma and Sid. I was going to dinner tonight but called it off, I'll have to go and let them in.'

'Good, I'll see you tomorrow, honey.' As usual Mike was gone.

Sid and Noma were waiting at the door, hands full of eskies and a big basket. 'Hello, Rachel, you won't come to dinner, so dinner has come to you!'

Rachel's eyes filled with tears; they were so kind. 'Oh goodness, come in, come in. I'm sorry I was so long answering the door, but Mike was on the phone. He thinks I should stay with Jane.'

'Not a bad idea; the only trouble with that is how long for?' Sid said this while helping Norma unpack the food.

'Looks like you think you're feeding an army.' Rachel observed taking in the huge casserole and two more containers that looked as if they were bursting with vegetables.

'Come on let's eat I'm starving, talk later,' Sid said.

Rachel nipped through and got out her last bottle of wine and before long they were tucking into the mountain of food Sid and Norma had brought. 'Now look, Rachel, don't take this the wrong way but Sid and I have both noticed you are getting thinner and thinner, I guess it's an effort to cook for one, so I'm not taking anything back with me. I'm leaving what's left over for you. I would have given it to you to bring home if you had made it to our place, so no arguments!' As she said all this Norma watched the emotions flit across Rachel's face, she was five years older than Rachel and a grandmother; her heart went out to her friend and neighbour. What a sad and lonely life she had now. She remembered when Rachel and Sam were first married; they had been so happy and full of optimism. Rachel had been a real looker and so full of fun, the years had worn it all away; it seemed so sad.

They sat for a long time afterwards talking cattle and gossiping, then Sid got to his feet. It was the moment, Rachel had been dreading, she stood too.

Norma laid her hand on Rachel's arm. 'Do you want me to stay, I can you know, Sid can come and pick me up in the morning.'

'No, God no, I'll be fine now. Please don't worry and drive back safely. Also many, many thanks for everything, I owe you!'

Rather reluctantly, Sid and Norma packed up and left after helping Rachel put the remaining food away. Some in the freezer and some in the fridge. Rachel got ready for bed but decided to sleep in the armchair, as she had immediately felt nervous when Sid and Norma had gone, though she was cross with herself for being needy.

At 3am, she woke with a start and with a racing heart, sat listening. She wasn't sure if an actual noise had woken her or if she had been dreaming. She heard one of the dogs' bark then, but a rather disinterested kind of noise, so in the end, she settled down again and went back to sleep. She was just so tired.

CHAPTER 30

When she woke the next morning, she felt sluggish and out of sorts. She had shared the wine but didn't think it was that. Maybe she was coming down with something. Then she remembered Mike said he would come out today and felt much more cheerful. However, when she went outside she got a rude shock. The gate to the hens run was swinging open and from a distance she could see dead hens lying around the place. When she got to the run, she found a piece of paper pinned to the door of the henhouse. *'This is just the beginning unless you move out.'* She gave a little groan of despair and gathered the dead bodies up. They would have been sleeping and easily caught and disposed of during the night. They all had broken necks. The chooks were some distance from the dog's quarters, and anyone approaching quietly wouldn't have been heard.

With a heavy heart, she collected up the carcasses and put them into a wheelbarrow. She would bury them later. She was angrier than anything else she thought, but sad too. They were dear old things or not really old, but They were part of her family, her animals, how dare someone do this. Someone, Johnny or one of his gang. Yes, he must be part of a gang she reasoned.

Mike didn't turn up until late morning. Rachel had been looking out for him first thing, finally given up and was busy putting the dead hens in the back of the ute deciding to drive out to the back paddock and throw them where the eagles could get rid of them.

Mike looked alarmed, 'What's this, Rach, what happened?'

'I guess this is Johnny's doing or one of his lot. They were all killed overnight, and they left this note.

Mike skimmed it. 'This is serious, Rachel, I guess you won't come back to town with me?'

Rachel shook her head. 'No Mike, I'm between a rock and a hard place right now. I'm scared to leave and scared to stay, but on balance stay I must.'

Mike took the two remaining steps to her and wrapped his arms around her; she buried her head in his shoulder. 'I can stay tonight if you want me to then we'll think of something, okay?'

Rachel pulled back and looked into his warm brown eyes. 'Mike are you sure about this? I'm older than you and you're still married and maybe it isn't a good idea. I don't want it to interfere with your job or anything.'

As an answer, Mike put his lips to hers and seconds later his tongue was exploring her mouth. Rachel felt weak at the knees but managed to say when he lifted his head. 'Mike?'

Still cradling her in his arms, he looked earnestly into her eyes. 'First of all, my wife has another man and they are planning on marrying soon; divorce is well under way. So I'm a bit younger than you, but it's not something I think or worry about. You are you, a very desirable and lovely woman, both to look at and be with. Thirdly, my private life is nothing to do with my job. Does any of that help?'

'I suppose, yes, if you are sure about all this. Yes, it helps.' Rachel didn't say anymore as Mike had other ideas and soon afterwards, they were enjoying their newfound intimacy.

Lunch was late, very late, Rachel pointed out there were lots of jobs wanted doing, but Mike said they needed to eat, and he would help with the jobs so it would be quicker. Rachel had her doubts about that as every little while they stopped and had a kiss and a cuddle, so jobs actually took longer. At one-point Mike said, 'We are as bad as a couple of teenagers, but who cares!'

Indeed, Rachel felt rejuvenated and almost danced around the kitchen getting supper.

Later, when they had eaten, leftovers from Sid and Norma's dinner from the night before, Mike sat looking at her. His brown eyes were troubled.

'Rachel, we need to talk, I don't want you to be here alone, it's just not safe, I've had an idea, I will get on the phone right now and see if it will work, is that okay with you?'

'What idea?'

'I'll tell you if it works out, okay?'

Rachel nodded. 'Okay, Mike, if you can think of something good, but I don't really see what you can do.'

When Mike finally got off the phone, he still looked troubled. 'Ideally someone ought to be here all the time, not just at night, but I've had a long talk with Sid and then Allen and they have agreed that Allen will come over and sleep here in the men's quarters. Secondly, I have talked to someone I know in Roma who will come and set up security lights around the place and who will also put a sensor on your front gate posts, which will hopefully trigger an alarm here, which will give you a few minutes to ring me or the station. Not the best solution I know, but at least it's something. I'm sorry sweetheart, I wish I could be here for you twenty-four seven but it's not like that, this job is a bugger sometimes.'

'It's okay, Mike, I understand about your job, of course I do, thank you for all of that.'

'I hope you always understand, Rach.' Mike still looked worried then getting to his feet; he cleared up the supper table. Not long afterwards, all thought of Johnny, cattle and Mike's job fled from Rachel's mind as she enjoyed sharing her bed with Mike the entire night for the first time.

CHAPTER 31

They were up very early the next morning, as Mike had to get back. He told Rachel to stay in bed, but she refused and insisted on making him some toast for breakfast, which he ended up taking with him as somehow parting was harder than either of them expected.

Rachel felt lost once Mike had gone, no chooks to see to and on impulse she saddled old Spot, her horse, and letting the dogs loose, decided to ride across her property instead of driving the ute. Then just as she was about to mount up, she had another thought and tying Spot up, went back indoors and packed herself a picnic lunch. Then she made sure that the house was secure, something she had never worried about doing before.

She checked cattle, cows and calves, bulls, fencing as she went, but she didn't hurry, she just savoured every minute. It had been a dry summer, but she still had feed so that was one thing less to worry her, then she had a light bulb moment when she realised that she wasn't thinking about selling up anymore and she was going to stay! Was that because of her relationship with Mike? She supposed it was, but it was deeper than that. She loved the land, she reckoned she knew nearly every inch of it, she was closer to Sam out here too, he'd have hated living anywhere else. The clusters of tall grey gums, the red soil and the blue, blue sky, it was just so stunningly beautiful how could she have ever contemplated selling, no she would stay. She rode on, finally ending up at the swimming hole. She took Spot's saddle off and left him to graze; she knew he wouldn't go far. She settled down with the sandwiches she had packed for herself and was soon tucking in. She hadn't felt this hungry in a long time. Must be Mike again she thought with a little smile. With her saddle as a pillow and her hat over her eyes, she laid back and was soon fast asleep.

When she woke, the sun had moved round so it was shining on her and she was hot. Looking about, she decided to have a swim, so she stripped off all her clothes and dived into the water. It was colder than she expected and made her gasp; however, she swam around until she felt really refreshed and climbed out. Then she had the oddest feeling, the dogs who were all laying in the shade and Spot, who was grazing nearby, all lifted their heads; Jasper, the lead dog, growled deep in his throat. Rachel, of course, was stark naked and shivered, was there someone watching her? She couldn't get dressed quick enough. She looked all around as she tried to scramble into her clothes. She looked around again; Jasper was watching the other side of the creek where there were thick bushes. The hair stood up on the back of Rachel's neck as she tried to get her jeans on hurriedly; as she was still wet, they were clinging to her. Finally, having got some semblance of clothing on, she called out, 'Who's there, come out at once!'

She wasn't sure if she saw a movement of the bushes or it was her imagination, her heart rate shot up and she called out again. Nothing, then Jasper and the other three dogs all started barking and would have gone across the creek only Rachel told them to stay. She didn't want them going off, if it was someone nasty, she thought she wanted the dogs by her side. Pulling her boots on she grabbed hold of Spot and saddled him up as quickly as she could, making sure she had got everything. Keeping one eye on the bushes, she mounted up as fast as she could and turned for home kicking Spot into a canter. She had to stop and open the gate into the next paddock but again cantered across half of that before she felt safe enough to slow down. Spot and the dogs were happy to slow down too and looking behind her, Rachel wondered if she had been silly, but then again, the dogs didn't normally bark at nothing. '*Oh, God,*' she thought. '*I was completely naked, and some pervert was watching me.*' But how could that be as far out as it is here? Was it one of Johnny's crew or maybe Johnny, but she hadn't heard or seen any bikes or any vehicle at all, it was very strange? '*I'll not tell Mike it would be too embarrassing.*' she decided.

Everything seemed to be in order when she got back, much to her relief and having had a good look round she couldn't see any bike tracks anywhere, though the ground was so dry and dusty, it would be difficult to see any if at all.

She had only just got indoors when the phone rang. 'Hello, Rach, where have you been hiding today, I've tried to get hold of you several times?'

'Sorry, Jane, just been out on old Spot, just riding round the place, making sure everything's okay.'

Jane wasn't really listening she had other things on her mind. 'Rach, it's your birthday in a couple of days, I know last year you didn't want to even think about it what with Sam passing away. But it was a big birthday so why don't we have a get together here the day after tomorrow, please?'

'Oh, I don't know, Jane, I'm getting too old for parties and it will mean leaving here and...' Rachel trailed off.

'Listen Rach, I wanted to surprise you, but that's not going to work, so I'll come clean. Mike and I got our heads together on this one and we're having a dinner at the pub and everyone that can come, is coming. It's all arranged so you'll have to come; you are the guest of honour!'

Rachel swallowed, the lump in her throat made it difficult to speak, finally she managed to say, 'What time?'

Jane laughed with relief; she had expected a bigger battle. 'Come here first say at 5.30 pm and we'll go from there, you will of course stay in town that night.'

After they had talked for a few more minutes, they hung up and it was then that Rachel remembered Jane saying she would stay in town, not stay with her, stay in town. Did that mean she knew about her and Mike being lovers? She shook her head at her own stupidity. Sid or Norma would have said that Mike was at her place late last night, of course they all knew. She was just mulling all this over when she heard a car and going out saw Allen drive up to the men's quarters. She went down to meet him.

'Hi, Allen, you are earlier than I expected.'

Allen was in his early sixties, been a drover most of his life, but in later years had settled at Sid's and was an unofficial manager. It wasn't his job title, it was just something he did when Sid was away, the two men had a lot of time and respect for each other.

'Well, I just thought I'd come over early, have a look around, get settled. The missus said you might not be here in a couple of night's time, but I reckon I'll still come and sleep here, if that's okay with you?'

Rachel tramped own on her emotions again her friends had been planning this for a time, she only just heard; she wasn't going to be here in a couple of nights time!

Muttering a heartfelt thanks, Rachel went back to the house, the generosity of her friends humbled her.

CHAPTER 32

The next evening when Allen appeared, he drove up to the house and hearing him come as she was in the office, Rachel met him at the top of the veranda steps. 'Hi, Allen, would you like a beer or something cold.' Rachel could see Allen had something on his mind.

'No thanks, I didn't stop for that I just thought you should know I drove the shortcut tonight and as you know it took me passed the old house. There has been some sort of activity there recently. Some of the bushes have been cleared away from the old shearing shed, and I could see a few footprints and tyre tracks in the dust.'

Rachel's alarm bells rang in her mind. 'Will you come with me and show me, Allen?'

Ten minutes later, they cautiously climbed out of Allen's ute, though there didn't seem to be anyone around, it was getting dark and the old, ruined buildings looked forbidding in the half light.

'I'll go first,' Allen said in a low voice.

'Okay,' Rachel whispered back, then wondered why they were whispering.

Treading carefully, they climbed the steps onto the veranda. Many of the boards were broken and rotted, part of the roof on the house had caved in but the end of the house where the chimneystack was, seemed to be in better order. All the doors were off and all the windows were just open spaces, detritus lay on the floor, except near the fireplace where a patch was cleared, and looking around, Rachel noticed a few tins of beans and other vegetables on a shelf to the right of the fireplace.

'Looks like someone's been camping here, let's have a look in the shed, I'll get the torch out of my ute,' Allen said.

He turned to go, and Rachel followed him as closely as she could; she felt very uncomfortable and a bit spooked.

There was evidence of an even bigger clean-up here, it looked as if nearly the entire building had been swept, the few old sacks and odds and ends that had been lying around were in a pile in the corner. In another corner were two folding chairs and a rolled-up swag, which looked in very good condition as if it was almost new. Looking round some more, they discovered a box with tinned food in it, not a lot but enough to last a couple of people a few days.

Returning to the ute they drove back to the house, both deep in thought. 'I think you should give Mike the heads up on this, Rachel, I'll tell the boss too, it might just be something innocent and nothing to do with your son and those troublemakers, or it could be some potential cattle duffers, who knows.'

Rachel had cringed when Allen had spoken of Johnny, as normally no one ever said what the situation was or had been that up front with her about him. Now she realised it helped her to know what other people knew and thought, she didn't have to pretend any longer.

'Thanks Allen, come and have a beer while I phone Mike then you'll know what he says and he may want to speak to you.'

Mike sounded worried when Rachel related their find, then asked to speak to Allen as Rachel had thought he would. She didn't stop to eavesdrop on their conversation and was disappointed when Allen came out to where she was sitting on the veranda and told her Mike would see her tomorrow; she had expected to speak to him again, but guessed he had a lot on his mind.

She was doubly glad Allen was around when she got ready for bed. The finds at the old buildings had worried her more than she liked to admit to herself, but once she got into bed and lay there in the darkness, all sorts of scenarios played out in her mind. Johnny, moving in by stealth and gradually forcing her out, scaring her out. An entire gang of leather-clad bikies, then it was a gang of duffers planning on stealing all her cattle piece by piece till there were only a few left. She told herself off for that silly thought as if she wouldn't notice! Then she thought of Patrick, had he come back but didn't like to show himself. But if he had, who was with him as surely there were two. Her mind kept her awake for a long time as first one idea then another chased themselves around in her head. She was dropping off when the dogs all set up a loud barking. As she scrambled out of bed, Allen's light came on as did the newly fitted security light down by the cattle yards.

Rachel and Allen met in the middle halfway between the house and Allen's sleeping quarters.

'Did you see anyone or hear anything, are you all right?' Allen was holding his rifle in his hand. Rachel hadn't realised he had one with him.

'No, not a thing, maybe it was a roo or something, though they rarely come into the yard, not this close at least.'

'I'll come back to the house and make sure you are okay. I wouldn't want anyone to have doubled back up there.'

Rachel looked at Allen in horror. She hadn't thought of that. Together they made their way back into the house and Allen insisted on searching the whole place before finally going back to his bed. Rachel pointed out someone could have gone down there to his sleeping place, but he was adamant he would be okay.

'Lock the door behind me,' he said as he left.

CHAPTER 33

After broken sleep and bad dreams Rachel overslept and when she finally crawled out of bed and looked down the yard, she could see Allen's ute had gone.

She sighed, she would have liked to have seen him this morning, more to recap on last night than anything else, but she knew he had to get back, Sid's place was bigger than hers and there was always a lot going on.

She decided she would leave after lunch and set about doing all the jobs straight away rather than have a coffee, the wind was getting up and blowing swirls of dust everywhere. A piece of white paper blew past the window and got caught in one of the bushes next to the path that led away from the backdoor. Rachel was about to retrieve it when the phone rang. It was Norma. 'Rach, are you okay? Allen was sorry to leave and not see you this morning, but they had an early start here. He told me you had a disturbed night but couldn't find anything.'

'Yeah, we did, but it was a false alarm it seems; I'm leaving for town after lunch, Jane's orders.'

She could almost hear Norma's smile. 'Sid and I will be there, it's all arranged, we're looking forward to it. See you later then, take care.' With that Norma rang off.

Rachel sailed through her jobs with a lighter heart than of late. She even put the discovery of the swags and provisions out at the old homestead to the back of her mind, and after packing a few essentials into her bag, she sat down to eat a quick lunch before heading off.

Sitting at the kitchen table, she looked up and saw the piece of paper in the bushes. She got to her feet and retrieved it. She didn't look at it until she was sitting back at the table, then she smoothed it out. In untidy writing it said, '*Hope you like my little present, Ma, it's nothing to what I might leave next time, so why don't you go while the going's good?*'

Rachel sat staring at the note for several minutes, trying to make sense of it; she knew it was something horrible, but what? Was that what had happened last night, had Johnny paid a visit and left something she wouldn't like. Getting to her feet, she went down under the house, but all looked good there; she searched around the house, nothing. There were no chooks to kill and the dogs, well she was sure Johnny wouldn't go very close to them. She looked at her ute that was parked out the front; it wasn't locked he could have stolen it, the tyres were all okay. She bent down; it looked all right underneath, as far as she could tell. She decided that when she set off, she would give the brakes a good test before she went far, before she left her place even.

A short time later, still worrying about Johnny's threat, she dumped her bag in the back of the ute and opened the door to get in. She didn't know afterwards what made her look down into the footwell but she did. Luckily, there curled up was a big brown snake, it raised its head as she recoiled; it wasn't impressed being shut in the car and was ready to strike. Rachel watching it, backed away, her heart racing, now it was free it slithered out and made off across the driveway to the long grass on the other side, it soon disappeared. How lucky she had been, she thought to herself later as she drove towards town. She had gone back into the house again after that and sat sipping a glass of water. If she had jumped into her car as she normally did or if the snake had been hidden from view, she would by now be suffering from an horrific snake bite with no help close at hand. It didn't bare thinking about. She had been around the house three times, paranoid that there would be an unsecured door or window somewhere, the house was as much as a strong hold as she could make it. The security guy should be out in a few days to install the sensors at the entrance, she hoped!

She drove to town much slower than normal, still feeling shaky from her near miss.

Jane could see something was the matter when Rachel drove up.

Later, sitting at Jane's table with a steaming cup of tea in front of her, Rachel recounted her near miss with the snake, she ended by saying 'some birthday present'.

'Oh, Rach, poor you, but how lucky that the snake was where it was and lucky you saw it before it had the chance to strike.'

Rachel nodded. 'I suppose Johnny must have put it in the car, oh, Jane, what a monster he's become!' Sudden tears threatened.

To distract her, Jane handed her a gift. 'Anyway, let's celebrate. Happy Birthday!'

It was a box with some expensive soap, shower gel, body lotion and hand cream in it, all beautifully presented. 'Wow, Jane, thanks, you didn't get this locally, it's amazing!'

'I got it sent, anyway you deserve something special. Now if you don't mind me asking, I take it you and Mike are, um, together?'

Rachel blushed. 'Yes, for now anyway, I've decided to take my chances, I expect he'll get tired of me one day, since I'm older and well,' Rachel shrugged, 'well, anyway if I can have a little happiness for a time why not?'

'I just hope you don't get hurt that's all, you really like him, don't you?'

Rachel nodded, suddenly the threatening tears were back and the lump in her throat made speech nearly impossible.

Jane hugged her friend tightly, poor Rachel, she thought she deserved to find lasting happiness, these last few years had been tough, even more this last little time since Johnny had shown his face. Somehow, it was wearing Rachel down more than Sam's illness and death, or so it seemed.

Like many women in the country, Rachel lived in her jeans or shorts, but she had fished out a dress for tonight, she hadn't worn it in a very long time but as she had lost weight it fitted her well. It was blue with a spattering of white flowers over it; it was low cut but beautifully designed so not revealing yet showed off Rachel's figure to advantage; she left her hair down and even put on a little makeup; she looked stunning, at least that's what Mike thought when he saw her. They had all gathered at the pub, but Jane had deliberately held Rachel back, so everyone was there when she walked in. To her embarrassment, there were loud cheers, whoops, wolf whistles and shouts of 'Happy Birthday'. It seemed everyone she knew was there. She was showered with presents too, from more soaps to tea towels, handstitched hankies, a gift voucher to have her hair done again at Gemma's; she was quite overwhelmed. When they sat down to eat, she found herself between Mike and Sid and they both kept her chatting away about cattle, the weather, many things they were all interested in. During the evening, Mike said in a low voice that he had a small present for her but would give it to her later. Rachel had changed and got ready for the evening at Jane's, but Jane had clarified that Mike was expecting Rachel to spend the night at his place. Rachel worried about this, as everyone in town would know. Then Jane pointed out that everyone knew where the land lay anyway, and it was better to brazen it out than try to be secretive.

The evening passed in a whirl of merriment and high spirits, then towards the end of the evening Bill, who ran the pub, walked across the bar room holding a big parcel wrapped in brown paper. 'Bloke left this for you, Rachel, I nearly forgot, it was a few weeks ago now.'

Silence fell on the room. Rachel paled, what had Johnny done now, but it was flat and didn't look threatening, so she reluctantly took it and with shaking fingers peeled the paper away. It was a painting of her house, with the sun setting, casting long shadows across the veranda. The tall gum trees to one side also cast long shadows, so the whole painting had a tranquil and happy look about it, some colours in the shadows were muted, while parts of the house in sunlight seemed infused with a gentle pinkish purple haze. It was an extremely beautiful painting. Taped to the back was a piece of paper.

On seeing the picture, Rachel had gasped and there had been a collective 'aah' from those that could see it. Now, with fingers trembling, Rachel unfolded the paper and read the message. Sudden tears filled her eyes. 'What does it say?' everyone was asking.

Taking a deep breath Rachel read it aloud, 'For one of the loveliest and most lonely woman I have met. I hope you find the happiness and peace you deserve. Love always, Patrick.' Now Rachel let the tears roll for a moment or two. She couldn't help it and she wished Patrick was there to thank him. Bill came across and patted her on the arm, 'Good bloke really but couldn't keep his booze in control, dropped this off after he had left your place, said he disgraced himself and thought this would make a good apology.'

'Thank you Bill, he is a good man but as you say he likes his booze too much, what do you think of the painting?'

Bill shook his head. 'I don't know much about art, but I reckon that's a very special picture; it's better than a photograph.'

Everyone crowded round to see, and all agreed it was an outstanding piece. Rachel re-wrapped it up carefully and went out to put it in the back of her car. She felt she was being watched in the dark car park but, looking round, couldn't see anyone. She couldn't see the figure dressed in black watching from the corner.

Soon after this, the party broke up and Rachel drove the short distance to Mike's cottage.

CHAPTER 34

Mike had gone ahead of her as she had lots of thank you's to say and gifts to gather up. She parked in his driveway and climbing the veranda steps. She was a little surprised that Mike wasn't about, although the lights were all on, she couldn't see him anywhere.

'Mike?'

'Come in; be with you in a tick.' Mike's voice was rather muffled, he was out the back somewhere.

'Do you want a hand?'

'NO, please just sit woman, will you!' Mike sounded slightly desperate. Rachel, though curious, decided to do as she was told.

A few moments later, Mike came in with a cardboard box, which he was struggling to carry as it was moving around in his arms. 'Happy Birthday, darlin',' he said somewhat breathlessly and almost dropped the box as he went to put it on the floor. Before either of them had a chance to do anything, a cute little face followed by a squirmy body and fat little paws wriggled out onto the floor. The little puppy was red, with two white paws and a white stripe down its forehead. Rachel dropped to her knees.

'Oh, Mike, Oh, Mike, what a little cutie, what's her or is it his – name?'

Mike laughed. 'It's a girl and your choice, your puppy, I hope you like her.'

'Like her, she's adorable! Is she a red cattle dog? What's her breeding, how old is she, where did you get her?'

'Whoa there, you'd make a good police investigator asking all those questions all at once.' Mike knelt down on the floor beside her. 'I'm glad you like her, she is ten weeks old, I got her from my folk's place, she isn't registered but you can if you want to. Her parents are good working stock and...' Mike got no further as Rachel put her lips to his and kissed him fiercely. When finally, they parted they found the puppy sitting looking at them with her head on one side. They both burst out laughing and the pup not liking the noise hid under a chair.

Mike the scrambled to his feet. 'More to come,' he said and went into his office, coming back with two envelopes. They were handmade cards from Em and Ben. They had drawn pictures on the front. Ben had drawn a cow and calf, which was very good, and Em had drawn Spot the horse with Rachel sitting on him. Ben's card simply said 'love from Ben' in very untidy large writing, with three kisses. Rachel sat on the floor with her eyes brimming; next thing, a little squirmy puppy was licking her tears away and made her laugh again. When she opened Em's card there were more tears as this one said *'I can't wait to come and see you again you are awesome, love Em.'*

'Oh, Mike, what can I say, your kids are the awesome ones, and so is this little thing, and you too!'

'You aren't so bad yourself, Rachel, I just hope you'll always think well of me.' Mike suddenly looked uncertain and worried.

'Why wouldn't I, have you got a string of conquests across the countryside I don't know about,' teased Rachel.

Mike shook his head, a shadow seemed to pass over his face then he grinned. 'Enough of all this talk.' And he gently pulled her to her feet. 'Now this little girl had better go to bed and so had we!'

Rachel's heart skipped a beat, Mikes words sounded exciting, comforting, loving, protecting too she decided as she let Mike take the puppy from her.

A couple of hours later, Rachel lay awake as Mike's breath told her he was asleep. She thought back over the evening, but mostly about the last few hours since she had come to the cottage. Mike's wonderful present, the children's cards and this wonderful man whose lovemaking was both tender and passionate and in those few short hours, had given her so much happiness. Then she remembered Mike's rather odd comments before they went to bed and how worried he looked. What was all that about? But she would not let them spoil the warm glow she had. Thinking this she drifted off into a deep sleep.

Mike woke, he had a security light at the front of the house, and it had come on and though away from the bedroom, some sixth sense had made him wake up. He got out of bed as quietly as he could and tiptoed through to where he could see out. He couldn't see anything, and all seemed quiet. Rachel's car was in place and so was his; he shone a torch around the area but could see nothing out of place, so after having had a good look he went back to bed. Slipping in beside Rachel, he couldn't resist placing his hand over her breast, which he could see exposed. Rachel immediately turned towards him. 'Are you okay, something wrong?'

'No, all good, go back to sleep.'

Rachel had other ideas though and rolling over she sat astride him and it was some time before they went back to sleep.

CHAPTER 35

As Mike wasn't in any hurry, the next morning and Rachel wasn't going anywhere until 9:30, they stayed in bed cuddling when they woke, which led to more lovemaking. 'Anyone would think we were youngsters all over again,' said Rachel when they finally got out of bed.

'You are young to me, Rach, and by the way you looked so beautiful when you walked in last night you took my breath away. I can hardly believe you fancy me; you could have anyone!'

'I don't want anyone, Mike, just you, and thank you for everything.'

Rachel bent and picked up the puppy who was snuffling around her feet. They hadn't forgotten her and had let her out during the night when they were awake. She had already taken a shine to Rachel determined to follow her about everywhere.

Having had breakfast Rachel asked Mike if she could leave Puppy at his place while she went into town, she was having her hair done and wanted to pick up supplies. Mike said it would be fine, he would leave her shut in the makeshift run he had made for her as he had had her nearly a week. Puppy had already had her first course of injections and Mike made sure she was micro chipped. 'She is still just Puppy till you decide on a name,' he said.

Rachel was beginning to run late so giving him a swift kiss, she ran out to her car and stopped dead. In red paint all across the driver's door, in huge letters it said, 'FUCKING A COP NOW ARE YOU, MA, YOU'LL PAY'. Rachel stared at it in horror. Mike came up behind her; he'd been going to wave her off. 'That's torn it,' he muttered.

Rachel turned to Mike and buried her head in his shoulder, Mike stood quietly just rubbing her back but saying nothing. When at last she lifted her head, she saw Mike had a strange expression on his face. 'Mike?'

'It's okay, now let's sort this out, are you game to drive down to the garage and get them to clean it, or shall I?'

Rachel felt rather surprised by Mike's reaction. He seemed more worried and uncomfortable than angry, but maybe that was because he was embarrassed. Rachel squared her shoulders. After all everyone knew about her and Mike. 'It's all right; I'll take it down, then walk to Gemma's from there.'

'You sure, love?'

'Yes, it's fine. I'll see you later.' Before her resolve weakened Rachel jumped in her car and with a wave drove off. Mike watched her go with a deep frown on his face. He cursed himself. His heart had ruled his head and now the shit would hit the fan big time. He returned indoors and got on the telephone with a heavy heart.

Rachel drove into Billy's garage feeling deeply embarrassed; it was the same end of town as Mike's place, so at least she hadn't had to drive through the main street.

Billy scratched his head as he surveyed the damage. 'It will take a while, but we will do our best, you staying in town?'

'No, Billy, I need to get back.'

'Are you sure mate? Seems staying in town might be a good idea.' Rachel realised everyone in town knew her problems, but she suddenly felt the need to get back. Goodness knows what was going on there.

'Please, Billy, do the best you can.'

'Okay, mate, mid to late afternoon, we'll make it top job.'

'I owe you one, thanks.' Rachel walked away as fast as she could, the threat of tears was back.

Gemma was chatty as hairdressers are, but she noticed Rachel was silent and asked her if she was okay or was she hungover from the night before.

'Just tired,' Rachel replied, then saw the smirk on Gemma's face; '*oh dear*' she thought, it wasn't that that made her tired, it was this cat-and-mouse game Johnny was playing. What was it with Mike this morning, his reaction surprised her like it had on Christmas Day, he was straight down the line wasn't he? She couldn't bear to think he wasn't but there was a tiny doubt in her mind.

'Sorry, what did you say Gemma?'

'Nothing much, I was saying that was a very good cheesecake I had last night.'

'Oh, yes, I didn't have that.' Rachel tried to concentrate on Gemma's chat.

At last, her hair looking far more beautiful than Rachel felt, she was free to walk back to the garage... Her phone beeped as she was walking back, it was Mike. 'Where are you, love, still at the hairdressers?'

'I'm just walking back to the garage to get the car.'

'Rach, I'm going to be tied up with work for some time, but I want you to stay in town, right? Just wait for me at my place, okay?'

'No, Mike, I'm going home, but thanks anyway.'

'For goodness sake, Rachel, I don't want you going back there just now, it's not safe, you don't know what Johnny is up to!'

'Mike, I understand you are worried but I'm going home and that is that it will be all right.'

'Rachel, no, I don't want you to.'

'Mike, I've made up my mind.' And Rachel turned off her phone. The worm of doubt had grown during this exchange and she was stubborn, Mike wasn't her keeper, she was worried and scared too but home she needed to go.

Bill was waiting for her. 'Sorry- Rachel, car still isn't clean we're working on it.'

The message now read 'ARE YOU MA, YOU'LL PAY'.

'It's okay, Bill, I need to get home. I'll bring it in next time.'

'Won't be so easy to get off if the paints older, are you sure you want to take it right now?'

'I'm sure, Bill, I'll pay for it when you've finished the job, is that okay?'

So having filled up with fuel, Rachel drove out to Mike's place to pick up her puppy.

The little pup was very pleased to see her. Mike had put a collar on her and supplied Rachel with puppy food and a harness for car travelling the night before. It took Rachel some minutes to get the harness on as the pup was a squirmy wiggly bundle, but eventually she managed. She was just getting into her car with Puppy when Josh drove up in the police car.

Rachel waited as she guessed what was coming. Josh was covered in embarrassment she could see as he got out of his car and approached her. 'Hi, Mrs Conway, um Rachel, Sergeant Grimshaw sent me to ask you to stay in town please...'

Rachel felt suddenly very angry. Who did Mike think he was putting Josh in this situation and ordering her around?

'Oh, did he indeed, well, you've had a wasted journey Josh, I'm going home right now.'

'I'm sorry, madam, but I can't allow it, you're to stay here.' Josh was red in the face.

'We'll see about that!' Rachel already had the car in gear and before Josh could react, she put her foot down and sped off down the road.

Josh watched her go for a few moments. He didn't know what had got into Mike who had told him that under no circumstances was he to let Rachel leave town. So, he got into his police car with the siren wailing and set off in pursuit. Rachel glanced in her mirror. 'I don't believe this!' she said out loud. Then as suddenly as it started, the siren stopped and looking in her mirror Rachel could see Josh pulling over. Mike had radioed him to see if Rachel was staying in town and on hearing what had happened, he told him to let her go. He could imagine that Rachel would be furious by now; he just hoped his worst fears wouldn't come to fruition.

CHAPTER 36

Her mind in a whirl, Rachel hardly noticed the journey back. The pup was good and eventually dropped off to sleep; it allowed Rachel's mind to go into overdrive. Everything seemed quiet when she drove up, and the house was as she had left it. Having given the puppy a drink, she made herself a cold drink and took it out onto the veranda. She sat sipping her drink and taking in the scene before her; the tall gums by the driveway, the cattle in the distance, the roses she had growing in the shade side of the house, the hills on the far horizon, they were little more than a blue smudge, but they gave depth to the wide blue yonder. There wasn't a cloud in the sky and as the sun lowered, everything was gradually becoming tinged with pink.

Pup, who had been investigating her new home, came across to her and Rachel picked her up. 'What do we make of Mike then Pup?' Rachel spoke aloud. 'I thought I knew him but now I wonder, his behaviour over the car and Christmas, why didn't he stick up to Johnny then, it's almost as if he's afraid of him.'

Pup just snuggled into Rachel's lap, having tried to lick her face. 'I know what I will call you.' The pup's red coat was catching the setting sun, and it seemed to glow. 'I'm going to call you Ruby, what do you think of that?' The newly named pup just stretched and yawned. Just then, the phone rang.

Rachel thought it was most likely to be Mike and wasn't sure she should answer it but, in the end, picked it up. It was Norma. 'Hi, Rachel, are you okay? Thanks for last night, we had a great time, though it was pretty late by the time we got back.'

'Yes, it was a really good night, thank you for coming.'

Rachel had been about to say more but Norma said, 'Look, Rachel, will you be all right tonight? Allen had a nasty fall off a young horse today and I think he should stay here for tonight at least. If he's no better tomorrow, I'll come across and keep you company.'

'It'll be okay, Norma, no worries,' as she said this, her heart was in her boots, but she didn't want to make a fuss. 'I hope Allen is all right.'

'He'll be good by tomorrow I think he's shaken up, we're none of us as young as we were!'

'You can say that again.'

'Mind you Rachel, you seem to get younger and younger, a certain policeman has done you the world of good I reckon.'

'MMmm.' Rachel didn't know how to answer that, she didn't know what to make of Mike at all. Though deep down, she knew he had her best interests at heart, hadn't he?

They chatted a little more, then ended the conversation.

No sooner had she put the phone down than it rang again. 'Rachel?' Mike sounded breathless. 'Are you okay? Is all good there? Is Allen there yet?'

Rachel didn't answer for a moment, she was gathering her thoughts. 'It's all good, Mike, but why did you send Josh to stop me coming home? It was extreme, to say the least, and embarrassing for both him and me.'

Mike was quiet for a moment then said, 'Rachel, you are particularly important to me; after the message on your car, I am even more concerned for you. I can't be there all the time and the guy who was supposed to put up the security sensor on your front gate has broken his leg, fell off a ladder or something. What I'm trying to say is you do trust me don't you? Come back to town for a few days, please.'

'Not tonight it will be dark soon, I'll be fine, I will think about it.'

'Please, love do, look I've got to go, see ya.'

As she put the phone down, Rachel reflected on the fact she hadn't told Mike she would be alone that night.

Despite her brave and determined words to everyone, Rachel was as jumpy as a cat on a hot tin roof. Every little noise had her heart racing and going outside with little Ruby was even more scary, but she wanted her to be house trained as soon as possible, as she was to be a housedog and companion. She was very responsive and would be very trainable, Rachel could tell. Rachel spent some time that evening teaching Ruby to sit and lie down. She was so attentive and eager to please; Rachel knew she had fallen madly in love with this little scrap already.

With her heart in her mouth, she went down under the house to the storage area and found Nellie's old basket. Ever since Johnny had raided the freezer, she was nervous about going down there at night. Back upstairs, she rummaged around and found an old, large cushion in the cupboard that had been in the office and settled Ruby in there. All this had helped her get through the evening and now she would have a shower and go to bed? No, she would sleep in her chair again; she couldn't face sleeping anywhere else just now. So, having showered, she put on her underwear and a top, found an old blanket and settled herself in her chair in the kitchen. She let Ruby have her basket beside her. The nights were getting cooler now, and she wasn't sure she'd be warm enough but didn't want to have the doona.

She couldn't get comfortable and tried to empty her mind and sleep, but she kept returning again and again to Mike and his reluctance to confront Johnny. He made out she was important to him but was she really? if so, why wouldn't he do something to help her? He hadn't said he loved her, perhaps she was just someone he wanted and now that he'd had her, his interest was waning. Stupid, stupid woman, why had she let him make love to her, he'd soon be tired of her, perhaps he was already. Then again, she had known this was a probability, but she wanted a taste of happiness if she had the chance, though she had expected it to last a little longer. Well, she'd just have to put up with it, at least she had a little pup to love.

Then, with a shudder, Johnny popped into her mind. However, she shut this thought down; nothing had changed really since he had reappeared, except he knew about her relationship with Mike. Suddenly she sat up. There must be someone in town that Johnny was in contact with because he seemed to know things that only someone close by would know. Who could it be? Something else to worry about. She shook herself and getting up, put on the light and made some tea, maybe then she would sleep.

CHAPTER 37

Rachel started; she must have dozed off. She looked at her watch, which she could light up by pressing a small button on the side. 3.20 am. She had only been asleep for about half an hour. This was ridiculous. Ruby was snuffling about maybe wanting to wee, that's what had woken her.

She pushed the blanket aside and picked Ruby up to take her out. Then she heard it, a roaring sound and looking round she realised there was a strange orangey red glow coming from outside. She had drawn the blinds and now she threw them open and gasped. The men's quarters were on fire. She watched the roof collapse. 'OH God' she said aloud and rushed through to the telephone. It was dead.

Turning around, she pulled on her jeans that she had left by the chair and an old singlet and making sure Ruby couldn't get out of the kitchen, she ran down the yard, but there was nothing she could do. The fire had too much hold. However, she turned on the hose and soaked the ground around the building, getting as near as she could. She didn't want the fire to spread. Suddenly, the hose was grabbed from her hands and Johnny was there in front of her. It was hard to see his face against the backdrop of the fire, but she could tell when he spoke to her, he was grinning.

'Want to put it out do you, Ma? what a spoil sport.'

'Johnny! How could you! Its dry it might spread.'

Johnny stood in front of her, a lighter in his hand, he kept flicking the flame, on- off, on- off. 'Thought the house might make an even better show, what do you reckon?'

Rachel stood rooted to the spot. He couldn't be serious surely. Finally, her voice breaking she said, 'Please no, Johnny, please.'

His demeanour changed. He was serious again, deadly serious. 'Now listen here, I've been patient but no more, you pack your bags and leave now, you silly old bitch, you hear me? The lads and me, we're in charge now.' He swept his arm in a circle and Rachel realised then there were many black-clad figures standing in the shadows. She had been too focussed on the fire and Johnny, to notice them before.

'Please, Johnny, I'm your mother, you can't mean it, please.'

Before she saw it coming, Johnny struck her across the face with the flat of his hand. She staggered and fell. Johnny stepped forward and stood over her. 'You silly bitch, of course I mean it, the old man and you treated me badly, you and him, you didn't give a shit. Always mean with any cash I asked for while you were all okay. He didn't even leave me anything worth having in his will, mean old bugger. I told you what I wanted, but you have been too busy fucking the copper to worry about me, so now I'm taking it and you can go to hell.'

For a moment, Rachel thought he would strike her again, but he stood back. 'Go on, get packing, you've got half an hour.'

Rachel got shakily to her feet. 'What about the cattle and my horse?' She was having a job to process all this, and her lips were swelling from Johnny's blow.

'This isn't a debate, Ma. JUST PACK AND GO OR I'LL TORCH THE HOUSE. IS THAT CLEAR?'

'POLICE, PUT YOU HANDS IN THE AIR.' A loudhailer ripped through the air. Then everything seemed to happen in slow motion for Rachel. She saw Johnny swing around as did some of the others, then he had something in his hand and there was a loud crack. With horror, she recognised a gun, and he had fired it towards the police. By sheer instinct she dropped to the ground, as all around her, hell broke loose. She crawled crab-like away back towards the house.

She was aware that Johnny had run and so had the others, the police were firing, so were the gang but it was dark and the fire was making the shadows jump around, then headlights came on from a police car, maybe. Rachel couldn't be certain as she crouched on the ground. She was only on the outside of the lights; they were facing away towards the fire. She could see figures running, and there were more gunshots from whom she couldn't tell. There was no cover near her, so she stayed where she was and hoped for the best. Then powerful arms were hauling her to her feet, and she was half dragged, half carried back towards the house. Her assailant/saviour had strong body odour; it wasn't Mike. She tried to fight but her position made it difficult; she flailed her arms, but it was no use. 'Stop fucking around, Ma,' Johnny grunted in her ear.

They reached the house and as they did, the police loudhailer burst into life again, *'JOHNNY CONWAY, YOU ARE SURROUNDED. LET YOUR MOTHER GO AND GIVE YOURSELF UP.'*

By this time, they had reached the veranda steps. 'Now listen here, Ma, do as you are told, else it will be the worse for you. I'm going to let you go, you walk up the steps in front of me or else I'll use this gun. Don't think I won't; I will, and I'll shoot that bloody police fucker if I can get a clear shot too.'

Rachel by now felt strangely calm, or maybe too upset to think at all, she didn't know, she just walked up the steps into the house like a zombie, Johnny walked behind her his hand twisted in her hair the gun held ready in his other hand.

Johnny slammed the door shut then went to the window, but not before putting the lights out. He drew back the curtains and looked out cautiously. He muttered something Rachel couldn't hear. Ruby woke up and trotted across the kitchen looking guilty, as she had done a wee near Rachel's chair. Rachel picked her up and looked round desperately for somewhere to hide her; she didn't want Johnny to see her. Too late, as she looked up from Ruby, Johnny had his eyes on her.

'What's this, another pup, we don't want that damn thing in here.' He made to snatch her from Rachel. Rachel stepped back anger taking over. 'Leave her alone, don't you dare touch her.'

Johnny smirked at her. 'Two silly bitches together, stay together then.' He turned back to the window just as the loudhailer burst into life again.

'JOHNNY, LET YOUR MOTHER GO AND WE CAN TALK ABOUT THIS, YOU ARE SURROUNDED YOU KNOW THERE IS NO WAY WE CAN LET YOU WALK AWAY, JUST PUT THE GUN DOWN AND COME OUT.'

'NOT BLOODY LIKELY, I DON'T TRUST YOU BUGGERS, I KNOW YOU'VE BEEN TRYING TO GET MY MOTHER ONSIDE. WAS SHE ANY GOOD? WAS SHE WORTH IT? IT'S TIME TO FIND OUT NOW ISN'T IT. IF YOU WANT HER SO

MUCH COME AND GET HER. LET THE ONE WHOSE BEEN FUCKING HER COME AND WE'LL HAVE A LITTLE PARTY. HOW ABOUT IT, MA?'

Rachel sat down in the chair. This was some sort of nightmare surely, this wasn't real, how could it be? The deranged man standing here threatening all sorts of horrors couldn't be her Johnny, he just couldn't.

It was getting light now, and Johnny moved away from the window. 'I'll have a drink now, Ma. Chop-chop, let's be having it.'

Rachel felt unable to move. 'You're closer to the fridge Johnny, help yourself.'

For a moment she thought he would refuse or hurl more abuse, but he opened the fridge and got out a couple of bottles. It didn't take him long to consume them. Rachel sat cuddling Ruby, watching him. She had many thoughts playing through her mind of things to say, but somehow the words stuck in her throat. She had said everything that she could in the past and none of it had any effect. Why bother now. The tiredness she had felt when Nellie died swept over her again. Why bother, why keep on fighting Johnny. He didn't care about her or the farm or anything worth having. Ruby could go back to Mike. Mike would tire of her soon anyway, there was no one else, except maybe Mike's kids, but they were far removed from her and would soon forget her as would her friends. She couldn't see that this would end well anyway so why fight it, if Johnny shot her, he shot her, she just hoped it would be quick.

Ruby struggled to get down suddenly, Rachel guessed she wanted feeding or letting out.

'Where did you get the mutt then, Ma?'

Rachel just looked at him and didn't answer. 'Oh, I get it, it was your copper mate was it, that makes sense. Well, we can have some sport here then, can't we?'

Rachel held onto Ruby tightly and started out of her chair. 'Don't touch her, don't you dare.'

'Oh, come over all protective then have we, we'll see about that.' Getting to his feet, Johnny raised his gun towards her; then suddenly there was a loud crack, the window seemed to fly onto the room and Johnny jerked and fell sideways: his gun going off as he fell, the bullet smashing into the back of the chair Rachel had just left in her effort to protect Ruby.

CHAPTER 38

Silence. Everything seemed to have slowed down and there was silence. Then Rachel heard screaming; it was her; she was screaming, she was still clutching Ruby who was trembling with fright and had wet both herself and Rachel. Johnny was lying on his side with blood pooling around his upper body. Then the door crashed open and the police burst in. It seemed to Rachel there was an entire army of them but in truth there were only three just then and one of them was Mike, though, with his helmet and body protectors, Rachel didn't recognise him. Rachel became aware that Johnny was moaning and almost dropping Ruby, she knelt beside him. His eyes were shut but as she knelt down, they flew open, he was still holding the gun and with hand shaking he brought it round towards her. 'DROP THE GUN,' the first policeman into the room commanded.

Mike was speaking into his radio, 'Doctor quick, injured man.'

Moments later, Merv came rushing in, he was wearing a flak jacket and obviously the police had got him there on standby. Mike gently helped Rachel to her feet and sat her back in her chair. She was shivering violently, and tears were streaming down her face. He prised Ruby out of her arms and sat her in her basket. Ruby was trembling too but sensed that she was safe and curled up and went to sleep.

Rachel was aware that Mike was speaking to her, but she couldn't make sense of what he was saying. Everything seemed to come from a distance. Then she was conscious that Johnny was being taken out on a gurney and Merv moved across to kneel by her chair. 'Rachel, Rachel, listen to me, Johnny is in good hands, let's see to you now. You're in shock love, and I think you need to go to the hospital just to check you out, okay?'

Rachel nodded, then stuttered, 'W-w-what about R-r-r-ruby?'

Merv looked puzzled for a minute then Mike said, 'Rachel's puppy. Don't worry, darling, I'll look after her.'

Rachel found herself being guided out to Merv's four by four and he gently settled her in the front seat. 'Don't worry about Johnny, he's already on his way to hospital. Now let's get you sorted.'

Later, Rachel would hardly remember the journey. Merv talked to her, and she answered automatically but didn't really take in anything he said. She just kept playing the events of the night over and over in her head. She was thinking maybe she should have done something differently, but what? Would Johnny have hurt her or Ruby or was it an idle threat? One thing was for sure, he had forgotten that the police were just outside and could see into the room, Rachel guessed.

When they got to the little hospital, Merv helped Rachel inside. The trembling had started up again and she felt woolly headed and weak. A kindly nurse came and helped her undress and into bed. She was given a warm drink; she didn't notice what it was, and finally she lay back and fell into a deep sleep.

The day passed in a blur much like the journey to the hospital, but later in the evening, Rachel awoke properly and found Mike sitting beside her along with another police officer Rachel didn't recognise. He looked older, profoundly serious and unsmiling. He was obviously a senior officer.

Mike was in uniform and it was evident this was an official visit. 'Rachel, allow me to introduce Inspector Taylor. He was in charge of last night's operation.'

Mike sounded very formal, but he winked at her as he spoke.

Rachel felt uncomfortable as she was in bed wearing a hospital nightdress, her hair was all over the place and her face felt bruised and puffy. The inspector held out his hand, 'Pleased to meet you, Mrs Conway at last, and I'm sorry it's in these circumstances. You will have to make a formal statement later, but I just wanted to have a chat with you now. Can you tell me the sequence of the events from your perspective last night?''

Rachel told him about being woken and realising that the men's quarters were on fire. She recounted the whole sorry business as best she could. She found herself crying and unable to go on when she got to where Johnny frogmarched her into the house and after silently handing her a handkerchief, Mike cleared his throat and said, 'Maybe we should take a break here for a bit, sir?'

Rachel interrupted before the inspector spoke. 'It's alright Mike, let's get it over with.'

'You'll have to go through it again, Rachel, formally,' Mike responded.

However, Rachel carried on and explained what happened next, right up until the shot rang out, breaking the window and hitting Johnny. She hadn't asked about Johnny; she hadn't really had the chance, and part of her was afraid. She didn't know what she felt about him just then, so wasn't sure if she would be relieved or sad if he had died.

Inspector Taylor asked more questions about Johnny's previous visits and about the buildings at the old homestead. Rachel looked from one to another. 'There is a lot here I don't know about, isn't there?'

Mike opened his mouth to speak, but the inspector held up his hand. 'That will be revealed shortly, Mrs Conway, when we have finished our operation. I would rather not talk about it at the present time. We'll keep you informed and tell you more shortly, but for now, we'd rather you stayed in town because your place is in effect a crime scene. I'm sorry for the inconvenience.'

'But what about my animals and I need some clothes, those,' Rachel indicated a small pile of clothes on the locker by her bed; it was what she had been wearing, 'are the only ones I have with me.'

The inspector glanced at Mike. 'It seems Sergeant Grimshaw knows his way around your property, he can make sure all is well, feed the dogs or whatever is necessary.'

'Yes, of course,' Mike replied, looking very embarrassed.

'I daresay you could bring some clothes in for Mrs Conway too.' This was said with a definite trace of sarcasm. The inspector looked even more formidable. Rachel sensed he was at the least, disapproving of Mike and maybe her too. It seemed he knew they had some relationship.

He stood up. 'We will be in touch later today Mrs Conway. G'day.' With that, he strode out. Mike too, had got to his feet.

'Sorry, Rach,' he said in a low voice. 'Better go, see you later, and I'll bring you something to wear, I promise.'

The nurse came in then, followed by Merv. 'Now, Rachel, we want you to stay here tonight then you can go tomorrow. You've not only had a traumatic time mentally, but that was a nasty blow to your head, so we think here is the best place for you just now. If you want to talk, my dear, I'm here, all right?'

The tears welled in Rachel's eyes then, and Merv pulled up a chair.

'How did it come to this?' Rachel cried. 'What happened to my little boy?'

'Well, we both know that the head injury he had as a small boy affected him badly, he had a personality change; and as far as I know, he was heavily involved with drugs these last few years. The police haven't told me much, but I have figured out that this is the termination of a big police operation to smash a bikie drug ring heavily involved with drugs. Johnny was a big player and a big addict too. I'm sorry, my dear, but that is all I can tell you and much of it is supposition on my part. Johnny is in hospital, he was critically injured, but he is young and strong so hopefully he will pull through.'

They talked more, then Merv took his leave, and the nurse came and helped Rachel out of bed so she could have a shower. She was surprised to find she was still very shaky, but once she had showered and washed her hair, she felt much stronger and even ate a decent supper when they brought her some food.

She had just finished eating when Jane came in and wrapped her arms around Rachel saying 'you poor thing' that brought on another bout of tears.

'Now it's all sorted, Rach, you are coming to stay with me for as long as you want, okay?

'Sid and Norma will make sure the animals are okay at your place, there is nothing you need to worry about just now. You just need to rest and get your strength up, I expect there will be lots from the police soon but if you want a shoulder to lean on, I'm your girl, that is, if Mike can't help. I'm guessing it might be difficult for him given the circumstances.'

Rachel nodded she thought so too.

CHAPTER 39

The next morning, Rachel was allowed to go to Jane's. Gemma's husband Steve wasn't working up at the Isa that week, so he came and picked her up. It wasn't long before Rachel found out the entire town were rallying around her. This had happened when Sam died, but somehow this was different, Rachel was incredibly grateful.

Mike phoned Jane's briefly and asked Rachel how she was. He sounded rather strained and consequently so was their conversation. Neither of them wanted to get too personal, though for different reasons.

Late afternoon, Jane answered the phone, and it was Inspector Taylor asking if Rachel would go to the station and make a statement.

When Rachel walked into the station, the first person she saw was Josh. 'Rachel, how are you? We're all so sorry about what has happened.'

Then the door opened and the inspector came out, followed by Mike who looked very strained. Rachel hadn't seen him look like that before, and it worried her.

She was ushered into a small room and invited to sit at the table, and the inspector asked her to go through everything relating to the night before last again.

'Now tell me more about your son, you say you hadn't seen him for some time until he turned up back in late August?'

'Yes, that's right. His father died the previous Christmas. I informed people I knew on the Gold Coast, as that was the last place I heard he was. We put a large notice in the newspaper, but it was August before he turned up. He never had intended to come to the funeral anyway, that was plain.'

'Was he alone?'

'As far as I could tell.'

'Tell me about the next time he turned up.'

Just then, there was a tap on the door and Josh poked his head around it. 'Could I have a word, sir?'

The inspector didn't look happy but got to his feet and went to the door. Mike who had been sitting quietly all this time, avoiding Rachel's eyes, took the opportunity and gave her hand, which was lying on the table, a quick squeeze withdrawing hastily as the inspector turned back. He looked grim.

'I'm sorry to have to tell you, Mrs Conway, but your son died twenty minutes ago.'

Rachel gasped and her hands flew to her mouth. She hadn't expected that. She had been sure Johnny would pull through and that maybe, just maybe, their relationship would improve. That wouldn't happen now.

'Do you wish to take a break and resume later?' the inspector asked.

Rachel shook her head. Nothing seemed real just then, and she was afraid when it did, she would be a mess. She just wanted to get this over with as soon as possible.

The questions seemed to go on and on but finally, the inspector stood up and turned off the tape machine having made a closing statement that the interview was over.

'You better escort Mrs Conway home, Sergeant,' he said stiffly.

Rachel and Mike left the station, it seemed as if they both had too much to say but didn't know where to start.

As they walked away from the police station, Mike put his arm across her shoulder. 'Rach, I'm sorry about Johnny, real sorry.'

'It's okay, Mike, it hasn't sunk in yet, I just feel numb. I don't know if I'm sad he has died or relieved. He was looking at a long jail term I imagine, maybe this is for the best.'

'He has been in jail a few times, Rachel, but it seems as if you didn't know.'

Rachel stopped and looked searchingly at Mike.

'You know far more about this than you've told me, don't you?'

Mike looked very unhappy. 'In a couple of days I will come and talk to you and explain, can you wait till then?'

'I don't suppose I have much choice, do I?'

By this time they were back at Jane's house, Mike leaned forward and brushed her lips with his. 'Promise to tell all then, take care, love, I have to get back.'

Rachel watched him go, the thoughts swirling around in her head like a whirlpool.

CHAPTER 40

Two days later, Josh phoned Jane and told her Rachel could return home whenever she wished. Mike had phoned her both days but had said nothing personal. Rachel no longer knew what to think about that. Though she knew police work was all-consuming, she felt Mike was avoiding her. She was angry then sad then angry again and told herself '*bloody men, who wants them?*' then acknowledged she did. She missed Mike more than she thought possible and felt surprised and disappointed by his continued absence.

Norma phoned shortly afterwards and on hearing Rachel could return home offered to come and collect her. Rachel had been trying to decide who she could ask, so jumped at Norma's suggestion. Jane had said she would run Rachel home, but it meant it would be late afternoon before she could get away. Shortly after Norma rang, Mike turned up; he had Ruby with him.

'Hello, darlin', here's someone who is missing you, well two of us actually.'

Avoiding Mike's out-stretched arms Rachel knelt down and fussed over Ruby who certainly seemed very pleased to see her. When she stood though, Mike pulled her into his arms and kissed her hungrily... In spite of her reservation, Rachel kissed him back with added fervour, though her lips were still rather sore. As they drew apart, Mike looked at her searchingly, 'How are you really, sweetheart, I can see these bruises are healing but what about inside?'

Rachel gave a wan smile. 'I'll survive I guess, but you said we need to talk Mike, I need to know whatever you can tell me about Johnny, the whole sorry mess.'

'I'll come over tomorrow and tell you, I hear you are off home today, will you be all right till tomorrow, tonight I mean?'

'Of course.'

Mike again kissed her long and deep, then he was gone.

Ruby at this point distracted Rachel by jumping around her legs and demanding attention.

Three hours later, Rachel was heading home. Norma glanced at her. So far, she hadn't said anything very personal but now she said, 'I'm sorry to hear about Johnny Rach, it must be so hard for you all this.'

'I just don't know how I feel Norma. Part of me is deeply sad and the other part is relieved. Does that sound awful?'

'I would have said it's perfectly normal, in fact if it was me, relief would have been my main feeling, I think. He wasn't a nice person Rachel, he was out to get what he wanted and it's hard to say this, but he would have got rid of you that's for sure.'

Rach nodded her head and looked out of the window, not wanting Norma to pick up the tears that were leaking out once again. Norma knew Rachel was crying so to distract her said, 'When is Mike coming out do you think?'

'Tomorrow, he said, when he can, I suppose.'

'I think he had a thing about you from day one, he was so insistent that Sid lent him a horse that day they came over to move the cattle, more or less ordered him to let him come.'

Rachel sat thinking about this for some time then said, 'Anything else I don't know?'

Norma shrugged her shoulders. 'Not really except Mike asked a lot of questions about you and the stud and Johnny, a lot of questions, but it's because he was keen on you, at least that's what we all thought, I guess.'

Norma was suddenly having doubts herself, thinking back Mike had seemed overly interested in Rachel and her property. Why was that because of Johnny?

As they turned into Rachel's driveway, Rachel found her heart was racing, what would she find? She leant forward in her seat as they crested the rise and started down the slope towards the house and buildings. Where the men's quarters had been was a blackened ruin of twisted metal and debris, and Rachel sucked in her breath. However, the building had stood slightly apart from the others and the fire hadn't spread, there were scorch marks around but nothing more. The house looked the same as ever, in fact from this distance, everything else did. Rachel took a breath she had been holding without knowing she had.

However, when they drew up to the house and went inside, it was different and there was plenty of evidence of the drama that had taken place. The kitchen floor had a big dark stain on it, the door was roughly repaired and the broken window was boarded up. Looking back outside, they could still see bits of police tape blowing in the wind. Rachel looked for her chair by the fire but it was gone, loaded onto a police low loader and taken away> It still had the bullet embedded in it.

Norma rolled up her sleeves. 'You go and sort yourself out, look round outside and make sure everything is as it should be and leave this to me.'

For once in her life, Rachel didn't argue. She found a change of clothes, then with Ruby snuffling at her heels looked around outside. There were lots of marks on the ground where the confrontation between the police and bikie gang had taken place. Tyre tracks, footmarks, flattened areas, where Rachel thought people had laid in the dirt. She walked round the burnt out building, then walked across to the home paddock. Old Spot, who was dozing under gum trees, saw her and trotted across to say hello. He had the paddock to himself but found it rather lonely, he was pleased to see her. Rachel walked back and let the dogs loose. Ruby was rather miffed, as she didn't like sharing Rachel with anyone else; however, the others didn't take that much notice of her.

Deciding she needed the exercise, Rachel thought she would walk over to the old homestead. The dogs all rushed ahead of her and when she got nearer, she could hear them all barking madly, as she came into view; she could see that they were barking at the old dunny which stood some distance away from the ruined house. It was overgrown and Rachel wasn't sure she had ever been up to it, surrounded as it was by thick bush. The only visible part of it was the roof, which was rusty, and an old brick path, which led into the bushes, but at one time, had led to the door. The dogs were all dancing around but seemed reluctant to force their way up to the building. Except Ruby, being small she had disappeared under the bushes that were covering the path. Rachel's heartrate rocketed again. 'Ruby, Ruby, come out, good girl, here come here.' Ruby ignored her and by now had disappeared. Rachel took a breath and forced her way in, pushing the vegetation aside as she did so. It all parted much easier than she expected and on closer inspection she could see that some of it had been placed there as camouflage. When she got to the door which was half hanging off its hinges, she stopped. The dogs had stopped barking and were all crowding around her. Ruby, being smaller pushed her way into the darkness of the old dunny, which was large compared with some. As Rachel crouched down to get past the door, she saw that there were scuffmarks and footprints in the dusty detritus on the floor. Straightening up, she looked round the small space; it had two old toilet seats side by side. At first, she couldn't see anything out of the ordinary, but as her eyes adjusted, she saw a rope attached to one of the posts holding the building up, the other end disappeared into the long drop.

With a racing heart, Rachel tried to pull the rope but whatever was on the end was too heavy for her and peering down it was too gloomy to see what it was. It didn't smell too good either, and it made her gag slightly. She decided she would have to tell the police and fought her way back outside. *Was there no end to all this*, she wondered as she hurried back to the house.

She outlined what she had found to Norma who had been cleaning the kitchen and trying to erase the blood, some of which was splattered on the wall, though most of it was where Johnny had lain on the floor.

'I need to phone the police, Norma, I'm scared what they will find, suppose it's a body.'

Norma put her arm around Rachel.

'You poor love, this nightmare seems to go on and on, doesn't it? do you want me to ring?'

Rachel felt weak and upset all over again. 'Please, would you? Thanks.'

Norma went to the phone which the police had repaired, and Rachel heard her speaking but didn't take in what she was saying. When she came back, she told Rachel that Mike would be there as soon as he could, though as it would soon be dark, he didn't think they could do much that night.

Norma looked at her. 'I'm sorry, Rach, I must get back, would you like to come with me? You are welcome to stay the night.'

'Thanks, Norma, I think Mike might come as you said and anyway I think I need to stay here and lay any ghosts, do you understand?'

Norma smiled. 'Oh, Rachel, you are one brave woman and stubborn too and come to think of it, independent. So yes, as it's you saying this, I understand. Ring if you need us and we'll come okay?'

Minutes later having waved Norma off, Rachel settled down to wait for Mike. At least she hoped he'd make it.

CHAPTER 41

Rachel was dozing at the table when Ruby started to bark in her little puppy voice. She jerked awake and looked at the kitchen clock. 10.30 pm. Mike wouldn't turn up now, what had upset Ruby, the other dogs hadn't barked.

Then she heard steps on the veranda but felt frozen to the spot. 'Rach?' It was Mike, she jumped up to let him in as she had locked all the doors and drawn the blinds. She opened the door and found herself enveloped in his arms, he was kissing her hungrily and all thoughts of what she wanted to say fled. Picking her up in his arms, he marched into the bedroom kissing her as he went. Rachel responded in kind, her need outweighing any reservations or questions she had. They undressed with eagerness, kissing and stroking as they did. When Mike took her nipple in his mouth, Rachel moaned with desire; wrapping her legs round him with a whispered voice in his ear, 'Please, Mike, please, I need you inside me, please.' '

Mike complied, taking her to new heights of desire and passion, that even with Sam she hadn't experienced before.

Afterwards, they lay side by side quietly and Mike said, 'Jesus Rach, that was amazing, you are amazing, I'm so lucky to have found you.'

Rachel was very, very sleepy, but she remembered why Mike had come out tonight and started to tell him what she had found. But Mike just said, 'Shhh, tell me tomorrow.' Rachel let herself drift away in a contented sleep.

The next morning, Rachel woke to find Mike already up, dressed and making toast. For a moment she was disappointed as she had hoped for at least a cuddle in bed, but then the memory of her discovery returned, and she was soon dressed and sitting at the table with Mike.

Mike looked very serious and worried this morning, he said, 'Tell me exactly what you found at the old homestead, it sounds as if it's something else that I should have dealt with.'

'What do you mean, Mike?'

Mike shook his head. 'You go first please, Rach, what did you find?'

So, Rachel told him exactly what she had found. 'Hmm, it sounds as if they have something hidden there that we missed. I'll radio in and let the lads know. We'll look now shall we? Do you want to come, or shall I go alone?'

Rachel shivered involuntarily but thought she would go too.

'But Mike. I thought we were going to talk.'

Mike put his hands on her shoulders and looked deep into her eyes. 'We will, this is just a loose end, let's get it out of the way first, okay.'

'All right.'

'Good, let's go Ruby can come too.'

Mike was in uniform and was in his police vehicle, Rachel noticed even though she had thought it was his day off today; however, she made no comment. It didn't take them many minutes to get there and Ruby got excited all over again, barking her little puppy bark. Mike went first, pushing the bushes aside. Rachel held back. She had put Ruby on a lead. 'Shit!' Mike jumped backwards. The brown snake slithered away, and Rachel was pleased she had Ruby safely on the lead. Mike turned his head. 'I nearly trod on the bugger, good thing he wasn't around yesterday when you came.'

Mike didn't creep in as Rachel had done. He got hold of the door and pulled it off its remaining hinge so they could walk in properly.

Mike stood looking at the rope for a few minutes then got his phone out and took pictures, then investigated the long drop to see what the rope had on the other end. It was too dark though and even with the torch light from his phone, it was too far down to see. 'All I can see is something rather large. Are you game to help me pull it up, Rach? Don't know what it will be.'

Rachel didn't like the idea much, she had been imagining all sorts of horrors, but she thought it was better to know than not, so stepping forward she got hold of the rope behind Mike.

'Maybe it's Shawn's gold.' Mike said, and they heaved away.

Moments later, the end of a trunk came into view. It wasn't huge but it was fairly big and had been lowered into the long drop endways, so it fitted in the hole. Mike got hold of the handle was on the end and with a final heave got it up and onto the floor.

Rachel gasped when she could see it properly. 'It's Sam's dad's old trunk, it used to be under the house. I hadn't noticed it was missing. It was stored away there with lots of other stuff, what is it doing here? Johnny must have done this. No one else would have known about it.'

Mike quickly untied the rope and, as it wasn't locked, lifted the lid. On the top were three guns, high-powered rifles and underneath were lots and lots of packages, all wrapped up in plastic, Rachel didn't need Mike to tell her it was drugs, she stood there with her hand over her mouth in disbelief. 'Result!' Mike almost shouted.

Rachel looked at him. 'What do you mean?'

'Tell you in a minute, sweetie.' And pushing his way back outside and through the bushes, Mike talked at great speed into his radio. Rachel meanwhile stood looking at the guns and the drugs feeling sick. It confirmed what Merv had told her in cold hard evidence that Johnny wasn't just a member of a bikie gang but quite a big player it seemed. Her blood ran cold. Her son was a monster, and she thought as she stood there looking at the guns and the drugs, there was no way he would have stopped at killing her if she hadn't complied with his demands. It was a very bitter pill to swallow.

Mike came back in, 'Come on, love, let's get you back; the boys will be out here soon to take this away and have a look around, though we had searched this area before. Obviously, not well enough, but searched it we had. Thanks for finding this; it makes my life a little better.'

'What do you mean, Mike? You keep talking in riddles.'

'Let's go back then I will tell you all I promise, especially now. Thanks to you.'

They drove the short distance back, Mike looked so much more relaxed than earlier, but as they got to the house, Rachel could feel waves of tension returning, She felt tense and she knew Mike did too, whatever he was going to say was big she didn't doubt that.

'I'll make coffee,' she muttered as they got indoors.

Mike sat again at the table, and picking up a piece of cold toast that was left on his plate, he pulled it apart with his fingers. 'Rachel, I'm not what I told you and everyone else I am. They sent me here to run this operation into investigating Johnny's gang.'

'Johnny's GANG!' Rachel spoke louder than she meant to. 'What the hell...'

'Let me finish, let me tell you all of it, please.' Mike looked very miserable.

'I was sent here because it was known the gang was moving away from the coast, inland and setting up an operation somewhere remote, though to start with we didn't know where. We have been monitoring Johnny for a long time and he has been arrested for drug dealing and such. However, we knew he was a big player, and it was thought if we could let him go and just keep an ear to the ground, we'd get him and his gang. I normally work undercover, but I had met Johnny once at the police station and they felt my cover was compromised, so I came here as an ordinary country copper. I don't think Johnny had recognised me in any case. It was helpful that you called the police the morning after Johnny had been here, as we had lost track of him the night before and weren't sure where he'd gone. We knew the connection he had to here but not the circumstances. I'm sorry I couldn't be more honest with you and tell you it was no coincident that we met or my reason to start with in taking such an interest in you and this place. However, as we became friends, it has made the complete operation much harder for me to stand back and to let everything run its course. The powers that be are not very happy with me right now because I have become too involved with you and—'

'YOU BASTARD, HOW COULD YOU?' Rachel leapt to her feet knocking her chair over. 'I THOUGHT I COULD TRUST YOU. GET OUT, GET OUT OF MY HOUSE,' she screamed at him.

Mike stayed sitting. 'Rach, please it isn't like that, maybe before I knew you, but not now, please, I don't want to lose you please.'

Rachel was shaking with anger. 'Just go, Mike, and don't bother coming back.'

At that moment, two police vehicles drew up outside. 'Your mates are here now so go, go on, go.'

Mike reluctantly got to his feet. 'I'll come back when I've seen to this.'

'No, I meant what I said, I never want to set eyes on you again, go.'

Looking stricken, Mike went out to his colleagues and Rachel sat down with a thump and buried her head in her hands.

CHAPTER 42

Rachel didn't cry, she was too angry and a little later, Ruby came up to her and asked to be picked up. Rachel sat staring at the puppy for a moment. Mike had bought her Ruby, maybe she should send her back, but the brown eyes looked pleadingly at her melting her heart. It was only a fleeting thought. Rachel scooped Ruby up and the little pup snuggled down on her lap. She knew her mistress was hurting and was trying to help. Realising this brought the tears and minutes later, Rachel was racked with huge gulping sobs. She couldn't believe Mike had used her this way, I even let the bastard take me to bed, what kind of fool am I? She was betrayed and used and never again would any man get close to her.

An hour later, a police car drew up in front of the house. Rachel had calmed down and composed herself, though it was plain she had been crying. Josh came to the door and knocked softly. 'Erm, sorry to intrude, Rachel, um, Mike said he had to get back, um, we've finished across at the old homestead, um, we'll be off now.' Rachel just nodded not trusting herself to speak and Josh hurried to the car. He knew that they had a blue but hoped it would be over soon.

A short time later Norma rang. She was dying to know what they had found. Rachel tried to sound normal, but Norma picked up immediately something was wrong. 'What is it, Rach?'

'The bastard, he used me,' Rachel blurted, the anger returning, 'how could I have been so stupid?'

'I take it you mean Mike?'

'Of course, Mike, who else?'

'Well, you could have meant Johnny, what's Mike done?'

So, Rachel recounted what Mike had told her, ending by telling Norma that she had told him never to darken her doorway again.

Norma was quiet for a time then she said, 'I think you are overreacting a bit Rachel, anyone can see the way Mike looks at you; he loves you. It was all down to him, the party we had on Boxing day, he wouldn't have brought his kids out to see you if he didn't think something of you. Then there's Ruby and all the other little things he's done. I think you are just seeing all the negatives, I'm sure he cares for you very much.'

'If he cared that much, he'd have been more honest, I'm sorry, Norma, it won't wash. Anyway, they found drugs and guns in the old dunny, so now you know. I'm exhausted Norma and have things to do, thanks for ringing I must go now.'

'Okay, Rach, speak soon, take care.' Norma rang off; she had known Rachel a long time and knew it was no good; she was as stubborn as a mule. There was no way she would listen to reason just now.

Lying in bed that night though, Rachel thought back over her conversation with Norma. She had thought Norma had been talking about Johnny not Mike. Maybe then, she was even more stupid and blind. Yes, blind she thought to herself, blinded by love and lust, no it was love she knew it was even though she was in denial over Mike's good side, she knew deep in her heart she loved him and always would. But she would never, never forgive him. He had used her as bait to get to her son.

Over the next few days, Rachel did what she had done before when things had gone wrong. When she had miscarriages, when Johnny was ill, when he was being difficult, when Sam was ill and when he died, the only thing that had helped her was hard work. Now she threw herself into work on the farm, she rode out on Spot and with the help of the dogs sorted the cattle out. She moved one mob from one paddock to another. She checked the windmills in the paddocks away from the creek. Although alone she somehow got the calves through the crush to ear tag them. When she came across the calf that Mike had helped birth, she found tears running out of her eyes. The little creature was so sweet, she wanted to hate her but couldn't. 'You'll have to go when you're big enough, you are too much of a reminder.'

Mike had rung her several times, but when his number came up, she just let it ring out, disconnecting the answer phone.

On the fifth day, she had only just got up and was in the kitchen making coffee when she heard a car, and moments later, Mike was at the door. He tentatively came in. He looked as if he hadn't slept for a week and was unshaven and dishevelled, much the same as Rachel, who wasn't sleeping either.

'Rach, please we have to talk, you mean too much to me, I can't just walk away, please give me another chance.'

'That's not going to happen Mike, I don't trust you anymore, you told too many lies and let Johnny get away with too much before you put a stop to him. You could have saved me a lot of the fear I suffered if you had taken him in sooner.'

'Don't you think I wanted to do that? My hands were tied. We had to wait until the right time when all the gang were together and the other night was the first time, but I tried to protect you as much as I was able.'

'But why didn't you trust me enough to tell me?'

'I wanted to believe me, but I was sworn to secrecy and in a way I thought it was safer you knew nothing. When that message was scrawled on your car I knew we had to act then as Johnny was aware of our relationship, luckily the entire gang was here the other night but we weren't quick enough to stop them setting fire to the shed and disturbing you. I wanted you to stay in town, Rach, remember? But I knew I couldn't stop you.'

Rachel was intrigued. 'How did you know and where were all the police, how come everyone was there?'

'Remember Johnny's sidekick Zac? he was our undercover man.'

'Oh.'

'We came in, or should I say the boys did, the night of your birthday and camped out in the back paddock where you found Shawn's body, then drove as close as we dared the night of the fire. Zac knew Johnny was planning something big, but he didn't let on to anyone what it would be, Zac was supposed to protect you if it looked bad, but he didn't expect you to confront Johnny as quickly as you did and well, you know the rest. Please forgive me, Rachel, Ben and Emma—'

'Don't you bring your kids into this; I won't be blackmailed like that.' Rachel's anger returned. 'It's over Mike, whatever it was, it's over. I don't feel as if I know you or trust you. Just go will you, just go.'

Mike took a step towards her, but Rachel put her hands up in front of her. Mike stood looking at her pleadingly, but Rachel held her ground and he knew then that she was too stubborn to change her mind. Rachel didn't see the tears running down his face as he stumbled back to his car and drove away.

Rachel sat down at the table, she was numb, she didn't cry, she just sat there going over everything that had passed between herself and Mike and also Johnny. She remembered the time Mike had come out and looked after her when Nellie had died but shut that thought down quickly. If she remembered the good things, she would waiver. This was best, she had managed without Mike before she'd manage again, she'd go back to looking after the farm and he'd go back to being a policeman, in any case she was older than him, he'd find someone near his own age.

Ruby came and asked to be let out. Rachel bent down and stroked the puppy, who was growing fast. 'We'll have to start training you and making you into a super dog, won't we?' Ruby wagged her tail enthusiastically.

CHAPTER 43

Two days later, Rachel had to go into town. First, Ruby had to have her next round of injections and Rachel was running low on supplies. She had spoken briefly to Jane who had rung her to see how she was but realised Rachel wasn't in the mood to talk.

As she drove into town, the butterflies started in her stomach. She wondered if Mike was around and if he was and she saw him, would she change her mind. As time went on, she thought maybe she should talk to him some more, maybe she had been rather hasty. By the time she drove down the little main street, her heart was thumping. *'This is silly, I'm too old to be feeling like this.'*

She drove to the vet first. Bob the vet was ready for a chat, wanted to know how she was, saying how sorry he was to hear what had gone on etc. Rachel hoped she wasn't rude, she wanted to get away and go to Jane's, because by this time her feelings had overridden her anger and mistrust and she wanted to see Mike. Badly. She would drive to Jane's and from there walk to Mike's. If he was at work well, she would go to the station, but she hoped to catch him at home.

Jane; was at work but Rachel left her car at her house walked to the bakery and waved through the window. Jane saw her and waved madly back, indicating she wanted to speak to Rachel. Rachel shook her head and mouthed later and, with Ruby on a lead, set off to Mike's cottage. When she got there she was disappointed to see his car had gone, the place looked deserted. With a feeling of dread Rachel walked up the path and knocked, knowing it was fruitless but wanting to make sure. The knocking sounded hollow. Stepping to the side, she looked in the window. The room was bare! She walked right around the cottage , and saw every room was empty. Where had he gone? She sat down on the front veranda steps feeling bereft; it was too late, rather proved he wasn't serious, didn't it? But deep down there was a little voice saying there was more to it than that. They had more going for them than a quick fling, or had they? She had forgotten what she had said out at the farm, all anger gone, she wanted Mike and that was that. Be easy enough to find him, he couldn't have gone far.

As she was sitting there mulling this all over, Greg Smith, the local real estate agent drew up in his ute and got out. Rachel very embarrassed got to her feet. She had known him a long time; he had made a serious play for her before she married Sam, but he wasn't her type, and he hadn't taken the knock back too well at the time.

'G'day Rachel, what are you doing here, want to see the copper do you?' The intonation he put on this made Rachel blush.

'I was just passing but there seems to be no one at home.'

'Nah, sergeant brought the keys round late yesterday arvo, said he was off. Two months still to go on the rent too. No skin off my nose, just came to check the place over. Want to help me?'

Rachel got to her feet; she had forgotten what a sleaze he could be. 'No, thank you,' she said icily and walked away as fast as she could. Greg watched her go with a grin on his face, he knew how to get under her skin, something he enjoyed doing ever since she chose Sam instead of him.

When she got back to the bakery, Jane was looking out for her and met her outside. 'Come and sit, Rach, I've something for you and I'll bring a coffee too.'

Rachel sat down with Ruby on the bench outside the bakery and waited, thinking how she would get in touch with Mike. She was surer of this than ever.

Jane came out with a coffee and an envelope. 'Mike left this for you yesterday, Rach.'

Rachel took the envelope from Jane, the feeling of dread churning in her stomach. With shaking fingers, she tore it open and read it.

'My Darling Rach,
I will always think of you like that because I love you so much it hurts.

By the time you get this I will be long gone, I realise now it was stupid of me to think we would still have a friendship after all that has gone on. You've had so much crap in your life you don't need someone like me making things worse.

You are a lovely, smart and fun person and deserve far more than a loser like me can offer.

I just want you to know that many times when I came out to your place it was nothing to do with being a policeman. I just wanted to be out there with you. I have stuffed everything up, my bosses have asked me to resign or take demotion, as getting so close to you wasn't a wise move, I could have compromised the whole operation. I was going to tell you when I came out the other day but somehow the whole thing went wrong; I said the wrong thing. I'm sorry. So, I am no longer a copper and have decided to go walkabout.

All I ever wanted is to be with you, protect you and love you, and I ended up doing the opposite. I hope over time you can forgive me, but maybe you won't, I wouldn't blame you if you never did. I'm rambling I know, but I am having trouble putting my thoughts in order, I love you, take care, I hope you find happiness.

Forever yours, Mike.'

'Oooh Mike!' Rachel moaned as she finished reading the letter. Jane put her arm around her.

'Bad news?'

Rachel handed her Mike's letter, Jane skimmed it. 'Oh Rachel, I'm so sorry, but maybe you can catch him if you want to, he only gave me this yesterday.'

Rachel shook her head, she was now feeling defeated, it was her own fault but maybe this was meant to be.

'He left yesterday arvo and it would be hard to know where he went, it's my own fault. I was too hard on him and blamed him for everything. Trouble is, I am still coming to terms with the whole Johnny thing, but I shouldn't have said some of the things I said, too late now. I have tried his mobile but it's switched off, it goes straight to voicemail. It's silly I know, but I don't even know where his family live, it's just something that we never talked about, the kids too, I just know they live in Brisbane with his ex.'

They sat a while longer, but Rachel was too dispirited to do anything else just then. She had the business of Johnny's funeral to contend with too.

Eventually leaving Ruby with Jane, she went to the supermarket then collected Ruby and drove slowly home.

CHAPTER 44

The following week, Rachel set off to Roma where Johnny's cremation was to take place. She requested just a few prayers before the coffin went into the furnace. She wasn't particularly religious, but felt she had done the best she could. Since the night of the fire, she had felt numb about Johnny. She didn't understand her own feelings and rather thought Johnny didn't understand his own either. Would he really have killed her, her own son? But it happens, she knew that. Did she still love him? No, she answered herself, she loved the memory of the little curly-headed boy, so full of mischief and sunshine, but he was long gone.

Her thoughts turned to Mike, she missed him so much and she had only herself to blame. It was a bitter pill to swallow. Ruby was becoming her constant companion and would wait outside the bathroom door or any other door that Rachel closed when she went through. She felt tired by the time she got to Roma, but it was getting near the time for the ceremony, so finding a shady spot in the car park, she put Ruby in the cage she had on the back of the ute and headed inside. The undertaker came and spoke to her, the coffin was already in place and Rachel took a pew at the front waiting for the ceremony to begin. Suddenly, the door at the back flew open, and a girl came rushing in. She was dressed from head to toe in black leather motorcycle gear and was holding a helmet in her hands. She saw Rachel and hesitated for a second, then marched forward and sat on the pew at the front but the other side of the aisle to Rachel.

Rachel, having seen her, concentrated on the proceedings at hand but decided to speak to the girl afterwards. When the coffin disappeared behind the curtain, she heard a sob escape from the girl and getting to her feet slide across the seat next to her.

'Are you all right?' she asked in a whisper. , knowing as she said it maybe it wasn't the best thing to say but didn't know what else to say in place of the rather silly remark.

The girl who had long blonde hair turned icy blue eyes on her and spoke loudly, 'Am I all right? Are you stupid or what? you're his mother and you ask me that! Of course, I'm not all right although it seems you are. Your fault he's dead, all your fault, you horrible old woman. Johnny said you were a bitch and you've proved it, got him killed, didn't you?' By now, the tears were streaming down the girl's face.

The undertaker was looking rather alarmed and came across, but Rachel held up her hand. 'I'm so sorry you are hurting, and I'm sorry Johnny got himself killed, but it wasn't my doing believe me, the last thing I wanted was him dead. Let's go outside and talk, come on, I'll buy you a coffee or something.'

Much to her surprise, even though she had suggested it, the girl got to her feet and marched ahead of Rachel out of the building. Turning towards her, the girl looked daggers at Rachel. She wasn't at all pretty, she had rather a sharp, almost fox-like face and several sores around her mouth, which was set in a thin line.

'You're sorry are you, well, I hope you rot in hell and you know where you can put your sympathy. I would rather die than accept anything from you.'

It was strange, Rachel thought later as she drove away, the girl's animosity had made her feel better rather than worse. Perhaps it proved to her that there was no going back even if Johnny hadn't died, there was no common ground, no empathy left/ The hate the girl had let her see could only have come from Johnny. Even though she was upset at his death, there was something deep seated and feral in the girl's eyes and her manner. It told Rachel that Johnny was far beyond any redemption and forgiveness. if she had tried to go down that path.

She stopped at a service station and letting Ruby out for a minute, looked around. A motorbike drew in and the girl from the crematorium got off and came across to her. Rachel drew a breath wondering what was coming now. 'Johnny had a ring on his finger, I want it.'

The undertaker had given Rachel a bag with a few things in it that had been taken off Johnny's body at the hospital. Rachel hadn't even opened the bag; it was lying on the front seat. She now retrieved it and found three rings and four studs, an old wallet and a few other bits and pieces. She handed the bag over. 'It's all yours, what's your name by the way?'

'Eve, not that it's your business,' She snatched the bag from Rachel and getting back on her bike, roared away. Rachel watched her go with a sadness in her heart. What could have been if Johnny hadn't turned into a monster...

CHAPTER 45

Rachel drove slowly home and felt exhausted when she finally got there. She had been going to stop in town and see Jane but was worn out physically and mentally, so she drove straight home.

She made herself some scrambled eggs and a cup of tea. The eggs reminded her of the first time Mike had made her scrambled eggs and the tears threatened; however, Jane rang, and they chatted for a bit, then Norma rang and again Rachel talked to her a little while. Just before she rang off, Norma said, 'A helicopter came over really low this morning and spooked the cattle, Sid wasn't best pleased. Are all yours okay or haven't you had the chance to look?'

'I was so tired, still am. When I got home, I just fed the dogs and didn't go any further, I didn't think to look, to be honest.'

'Of course not, you didn't know about the helicopter. I'm sure everything is okay our cattle soon settled down once the noise had gone. Some aerial survey, Sid thinks.'

They chatted some more. Rachel told her about Eve wanting Johnny's small collection of possessions the undertaker had given her. 'It's funny, in a strange way meeting Eve and her aggression has made me feel somehow less stressed over Johnny's death. I think it's made me realise how fruitless all my sorrow has been. Even if it hadn't ended the way it did, there was no way back, the little boy I loved had long gone. I don't think that deep in my heart I had ever accepted that until now.'

Norma was quiet for a time then said, 'I think that is great Rachel, that you feel better about that, why don't you try to find Mike and maybe sort that out too.'

'Well, I've been told that the inquest will be next week then sometime soon there will be an enquiry, a police enquiry that is; into Johnny's death and the whole operation. Apparently, that is normal. Anyway, I'm thinking Mike will be there, he will have to be. So I'm planning on seeing him then.' Rachel sounded more upbeat and felt it than she had since the shooting and fire.

Rachel went to bed feeling things were turning a corner. She felt safer going to bed, Johnny was no longer a threat and she would see Mike soon and sort that out. She admitted to herself she loved him to bits and if they could be together, that would be wonderful, though she was aware Mike may not want that sort of commitment. she wasn't really sure. She tried to think about what had been said but couldn't remember clearly. She had been too emotional to take it in.

She slept well but was up early; the mornings were chilly now and she shivered as she got dressed and upon going into the kitchen, lit the fire. Ruby was pleased and after going out to do her business, curled up by the fire. Rachel had only looked out briefly, but as Ruby came back in, she looked across the paddocks towards Sid's place. It had been getting too dark to see that far last night but now she could see the cattle spread out across the grassland. Nearer though was a hump lying in the middle of the paddock. It didn't look right and grabbing her coat, Rachel pulled on her boots and minutes later was striding across towards Spot who was lying inert. Before she got there, Rachel knew he was dead... They'd had a few light showers in preceding days and looking around Rachel could see where all the animals had run across the paddock in a hurry. She guessed it was the helicopter that had spooked them. Old Spot had galloped so far, then dropped like a stone. His feet had hardly paddled, he was pretty much dead when he hit the ground. 'Oh, Spot, dear Spotty.' Rachel knelt down beside him and stroked his neck. He was cold and stiff. Rachel's tears flowed freely down her cheeks. She'd had him since he was an unbroken, rather cranky three-year-old, twenty years ago she realised. Once he was broken, she hadn't really ridden any other horse and he had been one constant in her life when things went wrong. Later she would have to deal with his body but for now, she just sat beside him crying quietly and shivering slightly in the cold morning. She had known he was nearing the end of his life, but it seemed unfair he should go like this. The sadness, which was never far away these days, returned in force.

She didn't know how long she sat there, but finally, Ruby got fed up and demanded her attention. She had amused herself exploring nearby but decided it was time her mistress got up and did something else, so she jumped on Rachel and tried to lick her tears away. Rachel put her arms around her. 'Thank goodness I've got you, Ruby, please don't leave me as well, you are all I've got.' she said aloud.

The rest of the morning was taken up with the grizzly task of dragging Spot's body out of the paddock with the tractor, then Rachel turned her attention to getting the backhoe out of the shed. It hadn't been used since way before Sam had died, and Rachel soon found the battery was flat. The charger was too far away to plug into the battery and she couldn't get it undone from its place on the machine. It was stuck fast. She got very frustrated and finally got a crowbar and with a heave got the battery free. It was much heavier than she had expected, so it was the wheelbarrow to transport it to the charger. By this time, it was past lunchtime so she went into the house and made herself a drink. She wasn't hungry, the events seemed to have taken her appetite away. She slumped down in the chair by the fire and must have dozed off as the sun had sunk lower in the sky when she came too.

The battery was charged, so she took it back to put on the machine. Trouble was, it didn't want to go back on the same way it had come off. By the time Rachel finally got it in place, the light was fading. She started the machine up and going past the burnt up shell of the men's quarters and the house, she went to a spot at the top of the slope to the right of her driveway and dug a hole to put Spot in. By the time the hole was big enough it was dark, so she used the lights on the digger. She drove back and got the tractor with the chain Spot's body was attached to. It all took a long time and when she finally got Spot's body into the hole, she found the grave wasn't big enough. She sat still in the tractor cab, tears of frustration running down her cheeks. Ruby, who was beside her in the cab, licked her face and wagged her tail. 'You're right, Ruby, it will have to wait until daylight now.' Rachel clambered stiffly out of the tractor and limped home. All her joints seemed to ache, the temperature had dropped, and it was cold. She fed the other dogs, relit the fire in the kitchen and set about getting something to eat. She reheated some soup, had a shower and collapsed into bed. She was dog tired but found it impossible to sleep. She was realising that coping out here on her own wasn't so easy. She had always thought she could do anything Sam could do and maybe that was true, but some things needed two people. Should she see if she could hire someone to help? She shied away from those thoughts and at last fell into a fitful sleep.

CHAPTER 46

The next morning, Rachel rolled out of bed feeling weak and feeble. Thinking she was sickening for something, then realised she had hardly eaten anything the day before so made herself have a decent breakfast, though she hardly felt like it. However, it restored her, and she was pulling on her boots when Sid came barrelling up to the house in his ute.

'G'day Rachel, saw lights up your drive last night and figured something was up, thought I'd take a look, appears you could use a hand. Poor old Spot, he'd had a good innings. though, I guess.'

'Oh, Sid, thank you, yes, yesterday didn't go well at all.' Rachel told him of the difficulties she'd had.

With Sid helping her, it didn't take long to finish burying poor old Spot. 'Will you be getting a replacement, Rach?' Sid asked when they had finished.

Rachel shook her head. 'I can't think that far ahead Sid, sometimes I wonder if I should give it all away, sell up and live in town.'

'Hell girl, you'd hate it, I know Norma and I would, here you've got space. Everywhere you look it's yours, no light pollution, no traffic noises, no nosey neighbours, well except us I guess, but we aren't that close. What about your animals and your garden and things like that?'

After Sid had gone, Rachel mulled over what he had said. Would she be happier in town or was this the place to be? Where she knew the trees, the dips, the valleys, the rocks and the creek. The big skies and the endless views. Sometimes she felt it was so beautiful it almost brought tears to her eyes. Now the threats from Johnny had gone, she felt safe again, no longer fearful. That too made it harder to decide.

Later eating her lunch, she suddenly had a brainwave. or so she thought. If Mike's cottage was still empty, maybe she could hire it and spend time there and get a proper feel for living in town. Not that it was Mike's cottage, she reminded herself, he was only a tenant like she would be. Somehow, the thought of living there where Mike had been attracted to her and she went to the phone and rang Greg Smith before she talked herself out of it.

He sounded amused and as always tried a little flirtation too, but Rachel ignored him, telling him she was genuinely interested as he seemed to think she was just lovesick and not serious. 'Don't know where the copper went,' he said for about the fourth time.

'I know you don't, this has nothing to do with Mike.' Rachel was now losing her cool. 'I want to hire the cottage, it suits what I need, not right in town and it has a big enough back yard for the dogs.'

'Well, so long as you are not expecting him back, or some such I expect you can hire it.' Greg sounded very grudging.

'Good, I'll drop by soon and pick up the keys and do the paperwork,' Rachel said and hung up before she got cold feet.

A week later, Rachel stopped by and picked up the keys. The next day was the inquest. She had her swag in the back of the ute as she planned on staying in the cottage in readiness for the inquest the next day. That was to be held in Roma, so she had a journey in front of her. Norma had agreed to feed the dogs, but Rachel reasoned that when she was able, she would bring the dogs with her to the cottage. She was so excited she would see Mike; he'd have to be there. She had her hair done and then had dinner with Jane and her family.

Jane was worried for her friend. What if Mike didn't turn up or if he did, wouldn't have anything to do with Rachel, what then? Jane agreed to look after Ruby and the next morning, a by now apprehensive Rachel drove off to Roma.

She had found sleeping in the cottage rather strange. Before Mike had been there, some furniture went with the house so was still in place, even the bed they had made love on was still there, but Rachel found she couldn't use it. She unrolled her swag and slept on the loungeroom floor.

Rachel found herself a bundle of nerves the next morning as she drove towards Roma. Every scenario played out in her head. Then she had a thought and stopped and tried Mike's mobile. It was sometime since she had done that. She had tried it at the beginning but it was always switched off. Surely, he would switch it on if he was near town she thought. 'The number you have called is out of service,' came a metallic voice. Rachel took her phone away from her ear and stared at it. What on earth did that mean? Had he lost his phone, got a new one or what?

Feeling rather deflated Rachel drove on towards Roma getting there in good time. She hurried into the courthouse.

Two and a half hours later, she came out feeling deflated. 'Lawful Killing' rang in her head. But what really upset her was there was no Mike, he hadn't even been mentioned, not really. Zac had given his evidence behind a screen and his voice was changed as an undercover officer. it was prudent apparently. Officer Grimshaw wasn't called because he wasn't in the room or had fired the gun when Johnny was hit. As the inspector filled in the background to the case, it was deemed unnecessary to call Mike. Rachel had to stand in the witness box as she knew she would, but it wasn't like a trail The coroner was very kind and kept all the questioning as brief as possible.

Feeling it had all been an anticlimax, she decided to find herself a coffee before heading back. The police enquiry wouldn't be a public affair so she didn't think she would see Mike then either.

She had just started to sip her ridiculously hot cappuccino when a man slid into the chair opposite her. She looked up feeling alarmed. He had piercing eyes and was a big man, vey smartly dressed and clean shaven, he looked vaguely familiar, but she couldn't quite place him until he spoke. 'Mrs Conway. Rachel, how are you? Are you okay?'

'Zac, I wouldn't have known you until you spoke, I'm fine, well not really.' Rachel was fighting mixed emotions. The only time she had anything to do with Zac was the night Johnny and he visited her, and she had been very frightened.

Zac knew how she was feeling and gave a wry grin. 'I'm not the person you really want to see I'm guessing and I'm sorry about the night Johnny and I came out to your place and scared you. Wasn't much I could do except advise Johnny to go easy. He was one crazy guy.'

Rachel looked at him and decided he was genuine and no doubt brave to play the part he spent his life playing. 'I know.'

'Look, Rachel, Mike contacted me a few days ago and asked me to check that you were okay, he loves you and I know he is devastated that you blame him for everything turning out the way it did. Johnny played most of his crazy ideas close to his chest, and often we didn't know what he was up to.

The bosses weren't impressed that Mike got so close to you, it nearly brought the whole operation down. We had been trying to get the whole gang for nearly three years, you see, but they were very slippery customers. We wanted to get them all, not just the small players.'

Rachel sat fiddling with the paper napkin was on the table. She was close to tears but didn't want Zac to see. Taking a deep breath, she said, 'If you get the chance to speak to Mike tell him I'm sorry and that I would like him to come back, if he wants to that is.'

Zac got to his feet. 'I'm not supposed to be here, I will if I can but don't hold your breath.'

'What's your real name?' Rachel asked as he turned to go. He laid his finger along the side of his nose and giving a big wink said 'Zac, of course' with that he was gone.

Rachel sat mulling over the conversation she'd had with Zac and finally she started the journey home. An idea had taken shape in her mind, but she wasn't sure she had the courage to carry it through.

CHAPTER 47

A few days later Rachel took the bull by the horns and carried out her new idea. She researched the Grimshaw family on the internet; it hadn't taken long much to her surprise. They owned a large cattle stud, much bigger than hers in northwest Queensland. Having found a telephone number, she rang them. Surely, she could find out how to contact Mike. A woman answered the phone. 'Hello, Nancy Grimshaw speaking,' she said cheerily.

'Oh, hello, um, you don't know me, um, my name is Rachel Conway, I was wondering if you'd know how I could get in touch with Mike, um Michael?'

There was silence which stretched so long Rachel thought the woman on the other end had gone and was about to speak again when she said, 'Michael isn't here and we don't know where he is or even if he's okay. Can I ask what your interest in him is?'

Rachel was silent now, what could she say? All the things she had been going to say fled from her mind. 'Mike and I were friends, he was helping me when he could on my place, I... I have cattle too. I just wondered if you knew where he was that's all,' Rachel finished lamely.

'I'm sorry Mike called in here a little while ago, he said he'd left the force and was involved with some woman who had given him the push. He wouldn't really talk, he was pretty unhappy, we couldn't help him. He just said he was shooting through and that is exactly what he did.'

'Oh.' Rachel was now at a complete loss as to what to say. Again, there was silence as both women were unsure what to say next.

'How well did you know Michael?' Nancy asked after a bit.

Again, Rachel wasn't sure what to say, how much had Mike told his family and what relation Nancy to Mike was. His mother, his sister, sister-in-law, she didn't sound that old so maybe not grandmother. All these thoughts tumbled through her mind.

'Quite well, um, look I'm sorry to bother you, Mrs Grimshaw, um sorry.'
Nancy seemed to have shaken off any reservations she had.

'Nancy please, look I'm sorry I can't help you more, but are you by any chance the woman who Mike was involved with?'

Rachel found herself nodding then managed a whispered, 'Yes, it was all a terrible misunderstanding, I just want... I just want to tell him I'm sorry.'

Again, there was a short silence then Nancy said, 'I'm Mike's sister-in-law, his mother is very unwell just now, though Mike doesn't know it; we want to tell him about his mother, but over these last few weeks we have tried to get in touch, but he seems to have completely disappeared. All I can say is if he gets in touch, we will pass your message on. Should the worst come to the worst with his mother we will have to pull out all the stops and find him She is in hospital and we are just waiting to see. I'm sorry not to help you more,' she repeated.

Pulling herself together, Rachel thanked her and ended the call. It sounded as if they had an even more urgent reasons to get in touch with Mike than she had. She had made her bed, maybe she should lie in it.

CHAPTER 48

For the next few weeks, Rachel tried to put Mike out of her mind; however, now she had decided to live at the cottage part time, that wasn't so easy as it brought back memories. Also, she was having emotional episodes, she felt like crying one minute then almost happy the next and she would wake up in the night sweating, her periods were all over the place too. Thinking it was probably menopausal but not sure, she made an appointment to see Merv. He gave her a brief examination, took her blood pressure and felt her tummy, took her pulse then sat looking kindly at her. 'I think you're right, Rachel, you've reached menopause. It can be a difficult time for some women and some cope with it fine. You've had more than your fair share of troubles these last few years and that will, I expect, impact on your well-being somewhat. Now there is medication you can take if you want to, it will help you through this.'

Rachel's eyes filled with tears, she suddenly felt that life was over, she was past it, it was truly devastating, she wasn't really a woman anymore. Merv watched the emotions flit across Rachel's face and guessed in part what she was thinking.

'Rachel, my dear, I've known you a long time and been there through your ups and downs. Johnny, losing Sam, Johnny being killed, you've had so much to put up with as I said, but I really think you should look on this as a new beginning. At one time, you really suffered when you had bad period pains didn't you? Well, those will be a thing of the past, that's one good thing for a start isn't it? Look, I'm going to give you a prescription for HRT. Regardless, you don't have to take it if you don't want to but it will be there to help should you want it. Is that okay?'

Rachel nodded. 'Thank you.'

Merv watched her go a few moments later with a worried frown on his face. She had so much to come to terms with, poor woman and apart from friends no one to really look out for her; he was sorry Mike had shot through. He had thought he was there for the long haul.

To start with, Rachel just kept the pills close by, but one day after feeling very low, she took one and then another and soon she was taking them regularly.

She still had low times but, on the whole, felt better than she had for a while. The only thing was though she reflected she was definitely passed it now, even if Mike came back she couldn't expect their relationship to continue, she was going down the other side of the hill now and that was that.

She fell into a kind of routine, spending weekends at the cottage and weekdays out at the farm. She found it exceedingly difficult when cars or utes sped by, especially at night. She had some noisy neighbours too. As spring turned into summer, they seemed to continually have noisy barbeques. The dogs didn't like it either and a couple of times she ended up going back to the farm early.

However, that wasn't always right either as she seemed to be finding it harder to cope on her own. She could do most things herself but sometimes she needed a man and then she would ring Sid always feeling guilty. Sid never made a fuss about sending someone over, usually Allen, but Rachel was aware it wasn't always convenient.

She heard the enquiry was to take place, but she wouldn't be needed as it was an internal investigation. She did, however, drive to Roma that first day hoping to catch sight of Mike. When she got there though, she realised it was a futile exercise. Even if Mike was there it was highly unlikely, she would see him. She went to the coffee shop where she had talked to Zac and berated herself. She had made up her mind not to try and get back with Mike as she was too old and he was better off without her, so what was she doing there? Deep in her heart she just wanted to see his dear face once more, she thought answering her own question.

CHAPTER 49

Summer and Christmas loomed. Again, Sam's family were staying put and Rachel's father said he was too old to travel now. Jane invited Rachel for Christmas day lunch. At first Rachel refused but finally agreed to go. Christmas had turned out so well last year, she reflected, or rather Boxing Day had. She shut her mind to it.

Christmas day passed pleasantly enough, but Rachel found herself on the outside of things, It was no one's fault, she wasn't related to anyone there and although she had been friends with Jane a very long time, somehow, Christmas was different. On Boxing Day she went back to the farm. Jane had wanted her to join them out at the dam but she refused, feeling the need to be on her own.

This surprised her, was she becoming some sort of recluse or hermit? She hoped not. Once back at the farm, she regretted it as memories of the previous year came flooding back. If only she could put the clock back! She walked off across the paddock to look at the cows. All but two had calved by now. She found a cow that was obviously in deep trouble and she kicked herself for not paying more attention. She should have been here yesterday. Rachel set to work to see what she could do. Two little feet were sticking out, but nothing was happening, and the cow was very distressed. Rachel tried to drive her back towards the yards with the help of the dogs, but the cow walked a short distance then flopped down. She refused to get up. Rachel ran back and got the calving ropes. They hadn't been used since Mike had been here and were all stiff and dusty.

Going back, she felt around inside the cow and found the head, so at least it wasn't a breach. She got the ropes on the front legs and heaved; the cow strained. Nothing seemed to be happening. Rachel and the cow fought to release the calf, then suddenly whoosh a tiny calf slithered out, but the cow remained down and was still straining. There was another calf! Wait, Rachel said to herself there was a third leg, where did that fit in. The cow seemed to be giving up. Rachel looked round wildly and not knowing what else to do, ran to the house and rang Norma. She gabbled out her problem without waiting for Norma to properly answer the phone.

'Hang on, Rach, Sid or one of us will be there as soon as we can, okay?'

Rachel hadn't taken much notice of the tiny calf that had been born as she was too taken up with its mother. Now she could see it wasn't breathing, she tried rubbing it and blew into its nose but having looked at it closely she guessed it had been dead before it was born. She resumed trying unsuccessfully to help the cow. By the time Sid arrived, it was obvious that neither the cow nor her unborn calves would live and Sid put the cow out of her misery with a single shot from Rachel's gun she had fetched from the house. It was all very upsetting as it was one of Rachel's best cows, an excellent mother and always had good strong calves.

'I think there are two more calves in there and somehow they are tangled or maybe conjoined, only a caesarean would have saved them all, Rachel. Don't blame yourself these things happen.' Sid slid a comforting arm across Rachel's shoulders. 'Come on I'll help you deal with this while I'm here.'

'Oh God, Sid, it's Boxing Day! I'm so sorry I sort of forgot.'

'I hope you would still have asked for help even if you remembered, Rachel. The animals come first and so do you, remember that alright?'

This knocked Rachel's confidence to look after the farm even more and for a time she played with the idea of hiring a man to help her. Between Christmas and New Year, she moved from one mood to another, it didn't help remembering having Mike's children out on the farm and the fun they had all had. New Year's Day was a lot different to last year, she reflected, and different again from two years ago when she had just lost Sam.

A few mornings later, she woke up having had vivid dreams during the night though she couldn't remember them now. They seemed to be hovering on the periphery of her mind. One thing she was sure of was that somehow, she had made up her mind to sell up. Maybe a dream had made her decide but whatever it was, she was sure it was the right thing to do. She would sell the whole thing, the cattle, dogs, everything as a complete package.

Walking round as she always did in the early morning, she was making a mental inventory, after breakfast she would get a notepad and make a proper one. She was just clearing up in the kitchen when she heard a sound that made her heart race madly. A motorbike! She stood stock still, panic taking over; what should she do, where should she hide? Taking deep breaths, she went to the front door; she would meet this challenge head on, no hiding. Ruby as ever sensitive to her moods followed at her heels, her hackles up. As Rachel opened the door, the motorbike rider got off his bike and took his helmet off. Patrick!

He stood grinning for a few seconds then strode across and enveloped her in a big hug.

'Ah Jesus, woman, would you look at yourself, you're a sight for sore eyes so you are.' Patrick's lovely soft Irish drawl sounded so good to Rachel with her jangled nerves, she impetuously kissed him briefly on the lips.

Patrick's eyes seemed to glow with that kiss. 'You'll be making me think you're pleased to see me so you will,' he said still holding her loosely in his embrace.

'I was relieved you weren't some undesirable, that's all,' Rachel felt embarrassed now and extricated herself. 'Come in and tell me all your news.'

'Who's this then?' Patrick was looking down at Ruby who had grown into a beautiful young dog... her coat lived up to her name and she almost seemed to shine in the light coming in the door. Ruby, however, was looking at Patrick with some suspicion though her mistress seemed to think he was okay. The jury was out as far as Ruby was concerned.

Patrick settled himself at the table while Rachel put the coffee on and sat down at the table. 'Now tell me where you've been and what you've been up to,' she said. She was surprised how pleased she was to see him especially since he had left under a cloud, not a big one but a cloud, nevertheless.

Patrick seemed rather uncertain how to begin. There was something he was holding back, Rachel realised, as he talked about North Queensland and Alice Springs, some of the paintings he'd done and how they had sold. There was something else, something he wasn't saying but what? Eventually, he ran out of steam and sat quietly for a minute before saying, 'You've had a few problems, I was hoping to stay a while, but I see the quarters are gone.'

'Yes. They burnt down.' Rachel didn't want to relive that night; she was having nightmares enough without thinking of it during the day.

'If you don't mind me camping, I'd like to stay for a time?'

Rachel smiled at him warmly. 'You will be welcome, Pat, very welcome, it gets... I feel so alone sometimes.' The last bit come out in a rush it was something she didn't like to admit to herself never mind anyone else.

Patrick nodded and then smiled, his eyes twinkling. 'I promise to stay off the booze, so I do.'

Rachel smiled in return. 'We won't talk about that little episode, come here, Ruby, and make friends with Pat; he's going to stay for a while.'

Ruby rather reluctantly went and sat by Pat who fondled her ears and stroked her rather tentatively Rachel thought. 'You like dogs don't you, Pat?'

'To be sure, dogs are fine, I just have never had much to do with them before, that's all, she's a fine creature, wonderful colour, did you get her locally?'

Pain squeezed Rachel's heart. 'Not very local,' she said briefly not wanting to talk about Mike. She was suddenly worried Patrick would mention him and she didn't want him to, it was all too raw, she wanted to move on not talk about the past, it was dead and gone.

Patrick looked at her quizzically for a few moments then asked her where he could pitch his tent. Getting to her feet, Rachel went to the back door, Ruby following as close behind as she could. Patrick too followed, watching the dog. 'She's certainly not letting you out of her sight,' he remarked.

'Umm. How about here under this tree, close to the house and sheltered. You can use the toilet and shower in the laundry just inside the back door,' Rachel was determined to talk about the camping arrangements not Ruby.

'Looks good to me, me darlin', thanks.' Patrick was careful what he said, he knew much more about the fire and Johnny, and everything that had happened then. He wasn't prepared to let Rachel know.

'Is there anything you need right now, if not I'll leave you to it but come in and have lunch with me?' Rachel formed it into a question.

'Now that's an offer a sane man couldn't refuse, but as I'm not sane I'll say no thanks today but tomorrow maybe?'

Rachel was surprised by this but said okay tomorrow it was, but if he wanted breakfast like he used to that was okay too.

Patrick smiled to himself as he got his bike from the front and started to unload his gear, softly, softly was by far the best approach he felt, and it was working so far.

CHAPTER 50

For the rest of the day, Rachel found it hard to concentrate on her tasks. She was pleased to have someone close by; it seemed a very long time since Pat had stayed before, partly because so much had happened since then. She sighed; the downside was it made her think about Mike more. Ever since the fire she had been sleeping badly with vivid dreams, Merv had suggested counselling but it was something Rachel couldn't contemplate, she was tough, she told herself, she would get through it.

When the evening came, she decided to go and ask Pat if there was anything he needed, she knew he'd ask if he wanted anything, it was just an excuse to talk to him some more. She had only just come into the house through the front so wasn't aware that Pat was in the shower and got the fright of her life when he came out of the laundry door as she got there. Rachel let out a small scream and jumped backwards almost tripping over Ruby who was following at her heels.

'By Jesus, woman, you alright?' Pat grabbed her arm to stop her from completely falling over. Ruby, not liking her mistress nearly falling on her, gave a throaty growl and Rachel feeling silly burst into almost hysterical laughter. Pat looked at her for a moment then joined in laughing. Ruby glared at him balefully, she wasn't at all sure she liked this man. Suddenly, Rachel was very aware of the way Pat was looking at her, he was dressed, but his hair, which seemed longer than ever was clinging to his head in curly tendrils and his merry eyes were shining with mirth, he looked very handsome.

Pulling her arm away she said, 'Of course, I'm alright you just startled me, sorry I laughed, do you need anything?'

'Nothing to be sorry for me darlin', no, I'm good thanks.' They stood regarding each other for a moment then Rachel, muttering she had things to do, turned on her heel and went back to the kitchen.

Pat stood watching her go; it might not be so hard to get her to bed and be ultimately his after all. She had had a rough time and was a ripe fruit for picking if he played his cards right. He had decided that he was fed up, always on the move, he knew what had happened and had thought Rachel would be more open to his advances than before. If he could get her to bed, well, his feet would be under the table and he'd have a roof over his head, and all would be well. Rachel would have him to watch out for her and granted he wasn't really interested in the cattle or farm, but he'd help if he had too. It would suit them both he was sure.

As for Rachel, a small wriggle of unease started up in her mind, she remembered Pat's goodbye letter and his declaration of love, she didn't want him to feel she was misleading him, she loved Mike and that was that. She just wished she could tell him even if it was over; she hated him thinking she didn't care. She would have to be careful Pat didn't think she had changed her mind where he was concerned.

After an even more restless night than ever, Rachel was already getting breakfast when Pat tapped on the kitchen door.

'Come in, Pat, I've made some toast as before when you were here and coffee,' Rachel said briskly. Pat looked at her sharply, she sounded a bit distant.

'I have an inventory to do then if I get it done in time I'll be going into town. I expect I'll stay the night there then will you be okay?'

Pat hid his disappointment. 'To be sure, I'll be fine, anything you want me to do while you are gone?'

'I'm renting a place in town now and normally take the dogs with me but as you are here maybe you could look out for them, feed them etc.?'

'To be sure, no trouble, just show me what wants doing and I'll do it. Anything for a beautiful woman such as yourself.'

'That's enough of your Irish blarney Pat, come now I'll show you what to do,' Rachel spoke more sharply than she intended.

'What about the lovely Ruby.' Pat wasn't sure she was lovely, but he wasn't about to tell Rachel that, the dog was very wary of him.

'She comes with me.' Rachel sounded abrupt.

Shortly after this, Pat watched Rachel as she scouted around the yards and buildings making notes; he was dying to ask what for but refrained because he sensed she wouldn't want to tell him the truth.

Mid-afternoon, she reappeared outside his tented area; he had made quite a camp and Rachel was surprised when she saw what he had done in a short time...

'You look as if you are well organised,' she remarked as he looked up from a small canvas he was working on.

'Yes, well, I like to know where things are; what did happen to the place I slept in before?' Pat knew perfectly well but waited to hear Rachel's perspective. Sid and his men had helped bulldoze the remaining shed down and clear the spot so there was nothing to see just a big empty space.

'It just got burnt Pat, okay?'

'Yes, sure, sorry I didn't mean to pry.'

Rachel relented slightly. 'I know, now I'll be off soon. Is there anything you've thought of?'

'No, thanks, it must be quite a list you've got; going round checking everything.'

Rachel feeling she had been rather sharp and unfair said, 'I'm just making an inventory, I might sell the whole place lock, stock and barrel.'

Pat wasn't happy to hear this news it would upset his plans; however, he knew better than to say so.

A short time later having given Pat instructions for the dogs and saying she expected to be back late the next day, Rachel drove off, taking Ruby with her. Pat waited until she had been gone for a time then, thought he would have a wander through the house. He hadn't actually seen much of it, only the kitchen, he was a naturally curious person and Rachel hadn't mentioned the painting he had left for her. He wanted to know what she thought of it but couldn't quite bite the bullet and ask her. He felt she had changed since he had last seen her but wasn't surprised given the rough time she'd had.

Having looked everywhere and not found it, he only had the office left, but when he tried the handle the door was locked. He also wanted to know if Rachel was indeed hard up and that was why she was selling or was there some other reason. The papers might have told him, but it wasn't to be. He wandered round the veranda and finding the right window he peered in. There was also a door out onto the veranda, but it was locked when he tried it. Going back to peering in, he could just decipher the painting he had left for Rachel, hanging above the desk. It gladdened his heart and feeling more optimistic than he had since he first arrived, he settled down to await Rachel's return.

CHAPTER 51

As for Rachel, she thought about Patrick quite a lot as she drove into town, she wondered if his turning up was rather more than a coincidence. Did he know more than he was letting on? She was sure the bush telegraph would have spread the news of the fire, the drug dealing and Johnny's death, far and wide. Indeed, it had been reported on national television. Then there had been an earthquake in New Zealand, not a big one, no lives lost, but it took the attention away from the story behind Rachel, the farm and Johnny.

She sighed and turned her mind to talking to the delightful Greg. As the only real estate agent in town he would be the one to deal with to sell her farm. He was such a sleaze bag. Rachel didn't want to give him the job, but she had no choice.

Sure, enough when she walked into his office, he was extremely smarmy to the extent she nearly walked out again. In the end she said, 'Greg, if you want to sell my farm all well and good, but I don't need you to be talking all this bullshit, do I make myself clear? Save it for any potential buyers, okay?'

Greg looked at her hard for a moment, she looked incredibly attractive when she was angry, and she was one tough cookie he thought to himself, he couldn't help admiring her.

'Can't blame a bloke for having a bit of fun alright I get the message.' He'd seen the anger flash across Rachel's face.

They got down to business and having looked at her inventory Greg said he would come out in a few days for a look around himself and then get a package together for potential buyers.

'It's not often a place like yours comes on the market lock, stock and barrel. I'll advertise it as widely as I can,' he said. 'This hot dry weather won't help unfortunately; rain fall is down quite a bit from a couple of years ago.'

Rachel nodded. 'So far there seems to be plenty of water in the dams and creek, and I'm not having trouble pumping either, though I'm not using those paddocks that are away from the dams and creek just now. Sam was always careful not to overstock, but it's certainly very dry out there.'

Greg agreed, 'Your Sam was a good bloke, knew what he was about,' he said. Rachel looked at him in surprise, it was the nicest thing she had ever heard him say, he was usually so full of bluster she never took him seriously, but he had sounded very genuine.

Her throat closed but she mumbled 'Thanks Greg, see ya' and almost ran out of the door.

Driving down the road, she saw Jane coming out of the little supermarket and pulled over to speak to her.

'Hello there, here for the weekend? Why don't you come for dinner? Oh no dogs, just Ruby?'

'Hello, Jane, the dogs are at home. Patrick turned up so I've left him in charge.'

'Is that wise, he won't break into your wine cellar, will he?'

Rachel snorted a laugh. 'What wine cellar? I think there is only one bottle in the whole place, and I hid the whisky.'

They both laughed then Rachel said, 'Actually, I wanted to tell you before it gets round town, I should have let Sid know before I came in really, but anyhow I'm selling up, all of it, it's going.'

Jane looked at Rachel with round eyes. 'My God, Rach, that's a bombshell. I never thought you'd do that, well maybe a while ago, but you never said anything to let on you were even thinking it. Are you sure?'

'I'm sure, look can we talk over dinner, I need to go and open up the cottage and things like that okay?'

'Sure, see you later.' Jane watched her friend drive away with a puzzled expression on her face. She didn't know what to think. Rachel seemed so full of surprises and mood swings, she was beginning to think she didn't know her friend as well as she thought.

When Rachel turned up a little later clutching a bottle of wine, she seemed very upbeat but in a way that made Jane think she was putting on an act. Indeed she was, as alone in the cottage she had suddenly been overcome with memories of Mike and how he'd loved being out with her; seeing to the cattle, mending fences, checking the pumps, feeding the dogs. Their last night together in the cottage, how he had made such tender love to her and given her Ruby. For much of the time since their last encounter, Rachel had managed to keep those memories buried, not completely but enough so she could cope. Perhaps it was because Patrick had turned up again but suddenly thoughts of Mike seemed to be filling her head and tugging at her heartstrings.

For much of the time they just talked local gossip and weather, not touching on the bigger issues until nearing the end of the meal.

Ben said, 'Jane tells me you've put the farm on the market, the whole lot, do you really want to sell up like that, animals, equipment, house, the whole works in one fell swoop?'

Jane shifted in her chair uncomfortably; she'd asked Ben not to say much. Rachel's hackles rose as it didn't take much these days to make her angry. 'Yes, Ben. Not that's it's any of your business, it's exactly what I intend to do.'

Seeing the dangerous gleam in her eye Ben backed down. 'Okay, well, I suppose you know what you're doing.'

Rachel looked at him coldly. 'There is no SUPPOSE ABOUT IT, I KNOW EXACTLY WHAT I'M DOING.' Realising she was shouting; she lowered her voice. 'Sorry, can we talk about something else.'

The rest of the meal passed with them all feeling awkward. Jane had never seen her friend like that, and Rachel was ashamed she had lost her temper. Ben and the girls were astonished too; they had never seen Rachel like this. Emotional and weepy, yes, but not this anger, which had come from nowhere.

Later lying in bed Ben said, 'I'm sorry Jane, I didn't mean to upset Rachel.'

Jane turned and laid her head on Ben's shoulder snuggling up to him. 'I know you didn't. I think the strain of the last two years is only now starting to affect her. She came through losing Sam well really, but then, there was Johnny and all his threats, then Mike, then losing both Johnny and Mike. Johnny was her son after all but Mike, well, she loved him and still does, I think. Trouble is she doesn't talk about her problems now. She did when Sam was dying, but now, she shuts down and bottles it all up, it's not good.'

Rachel, back at the cottage sat in the chair by the window looking out at the starlit night. She had got in the habit of doing this as the bedroom stirred up too many memories., Tonight they were at the forefront of her mind anyway. '*Oh God, why did I go off at Ben like that? They have been so good to me and so patient through all my ups and downs.*' Tears threatened but she swallowed angrily, she wouldn't give in to them or she'd never stop.

CHAPTER 52

Before she left the next morning, Rachel bought the biggest box of chocolates from the supermarket and going round the back of the pub she persuaded Jim the publican to let her have three bottles of wine. Jane was busy in the bakery when Rachel got there so she just told Jane there was something for her and Ben out the back, not to leave it too long, then was gone before Jane had a chance to react.

When she got home, there was no sign of Pat, so she made herself some coffee and took it out onto the veranda. Just then, the phone rang. It was Norma, they chatted for a moment or two then Norma said, 'I'll come straight to the point, Rach, the rumour about is that you are selling up, is that true?'

'The bush telegraph has been busy, yes, Norma, I've had enough of struggling on my own.'

'Ah, Rachel, you know we're here if you want us! What will you do, where will you go? I can't see you living in town and you're such a doer, you'll get bored without something to do. You love your cattle too and your home and—'

'Stop please Norma, I know all this, I just feel I can't cope any more on my own, alright?'

Norma said no more about it, she changed the subject making some trivial remark about the dogs. Rachel was grateful and a few minutes later, ended the conversation with a promise to pop over soon and see Norma.

Rachel did a tour of the cattle in the ute, her mind buzzing. Norma had touched a raw nerve. Rachel wasn't sure herself what she would do, the property had been her life's work and she couldn't see herself doing anything else. Yes, she loved gardening but knew it wouldn't fill her hours long enough. Living in town? She wasn't sure she could do that either as just people driving past seemed strange, maybe she would get used to that. She liked reading but only up to a point. She didn't really sew, only if she had to; she didn't knit or paint or have any hobbies she could really think of. Working alongside Sam had been enough, all she had wanted. The cattle, the horses, dogs, the wide-open spaces and huge skies, the graceful gums and the creek glistening in the sun. Tears pooled suddenly in her eyes. She rubbed Ruby's head. 'I'm damned if I do and damned if I don't it seems, Rube,' she said.

Pat didn't appear until Rachel was getting her supper ready, he stuck his head round the kitchen door and just said hello and he'd see her in the morning. Rachel wasn't that sorry; she didn't feel like talking to anyone just then.

A couple of days passed then Greg came out to have a look around and finalise with Rachel the sale package. Rachel felt drained when he had gone. She hadn't seen much of Pat either and wondered if he was avoiding her. That evening though Pat came and tapped on the kitchen door. He'd just had a shower and a rather close shave, Rachel guessed as he had a couple of pieces of tissue stuck to his face.

'How's the most beautiful girl I know?' he asked cheekily.

'Okay, thanks, Pat, I haven't seen you for a day or two not even breakfast.'

'Well, I'm guessing you have a lot on your plate, me darlin', so I thought I'd give you some space.'

'Okay,' Rachel thought for a split second then said, 'would you like to eat with me, it's about ready and there's enough for two.'

Pat hesitated for a moment then said, 'To be sure I'd like that. I get fed up with my own cooking, so I do.'

'No offence, Pat, but I think we might stick to water,' Rachel said a few moments later as they sat down...

Pat shrugged then grinned at her. 'You've got the measure of me so you have, I think it's safer.'

Rachel laughed at this and relaxed, she felt more relaxed in Pat's company now he wouldn't judge her, she thought to herself.

The evening passed very pleasantly, Pat regaling her with stories about what he had done after he left her place before and places and people he had encountered.

'I was going to go down the Gibb River Road but thought better of it,' he said.

'What put you off then?' Rachel had heard it was a very rough route but spectacular too.

Suddenly, Pat looked uncomfortable. 'Aw, just some guy I met, nothing really.' He sat quiet then, as if he'd said something he didn't want to or hadn't meant to.

The silence stretched then realising he wasn't going to say more and understanding as she felt like that quite a few times especially lately, Rachel got to her feet.

'Tea? Coffee?'

'Ahh, be Jesus, woman, you make a grand cup of coffee so you do, how could a man refuse such an offer?'

Rachel smiled and set about making coffee but had seen the look of relief on Pat's face, what was that about?

The next day, Pat spent the day in and around his camp and popped in a few times with rather flimsy excuses, Rachel looked at him oddly the third time it happened.

In the end coming in from the veggie garden where she had been preparing the soil for more plants she said, 'Pat, what is it you want to say, you're like a cat on a hot tin roof.'

'Rachel, I'm sorry but do you think you are doing the right thing selling up?' It wasn't at all what he wanted to say but it would do for now.

Rachel though was annoyed. 'Why don't you and everyone else mind their own bloody business?'

Pat looked crestfallen then drawing a breath, he said he was sorry and started to walk away. Then turned back, opened his mouth then walked away again. Rachel stood watching him, what an earth was the matter. Anyone would think he was afraid of her.

It was quite late that evening when Pat tapped on the door. 'Can I have a word, Rachel, please,' he sounded serious and formal.

Rachel sighed. 'Make it quick then, I am just off to bed.'

Pat stepped up close to her and looking at her in the eyes said, 'That sounds a bit like an offer.' Before Rachel had time to react, he pulled her into his arms and kissed her passionately, his hands finding their way under her shirt at her back and caressing her bare skin. Although he had made a pass at her before Rachel was caught completely off balance and stood still, not responding but not rejecting either. He deftly unhooked her bra with one hand and then Rachel woke up and shoved him away.

'What the hell do you think you are doing? Get off me!' Rachel was angry, she didn't need this.

'I'm sorry, I thought maybe you were lonely, a bit of a tumble between the sheets might be good for both of us.'

'We've been here before, Pat, the answer is no.'

He stood looking at her then muttering sorry again, disappeared outside.

Rachel sat down at the table and put her head in her hands, why was everything so complicated?

CHAPTER 53

The next morning, Rachel had hardly got into the kitchen when Pat appeared. 'Coffee?' she asked him hoping to show she didn't bear a grudge, she rather thought he would leave again now.

'Please.' Pat sat down; he didn't look as if he'd slept much.

'I have something to tell you, or rather confess, please sit down and listen.'

'You know I mentioned the Gibb River Road, well, the guy I met who told me about it was Mike.'

'Mike,' Rachel's heart leapt, 'you saw Mike, how was he? Was he okay where exactly was he?'

'Whoa, just let me tell you in my own time, okay?'

Her heart thudding away in her chest, Rachel almost thought she couldn't breathe, but she sat down on shaky legs and whispered, 'Yes, go ahead.'

'Well, after I left here I was a bit sorry for myself, I really think an awful lot of you, I've never met anyone who comes near my ideal woman, you seem to fit the mould... No, let me speak.' Rachel had wanted to interrupt him.

'So, I wandered here and there, painting a bit, picking up odd jobs, what I've always done really. Then I found myself up near Broome in the end but out in the sticks, not in town, found a quiet beach and camped just behind it. One day this rough looking ute drove up to the edge of the place where I was. It had seen better days and so had the bloke who got out, long hair unshaven but somehow familiar. I was painting, had set my easel up and there I was wondering where I'd seen him before. After a bit, he came over then I recognised him as he did me at the same time, it was Mike. He'd just driven the Gibb River Road and had had a blow out and a generally bad time, it's pretty rough that route at times. Anyway, to cut to the chase, we camped together for a bit. He told me what had happened and how you told him to get lost, made me reckon I might have a chance, that's why I came back. But you still love him, don't you?'

Rachel nodded unable to speak. Pat continued, 'He told me he'd fucked everything in his life up. His marriage, his career, and his relationship with you. He hadn't seen his kids either since he left, he threw his phone away and hasn't been in contact with anyone he knows, his family or anyone. He said he loved you more than anything else and as you didn't want him he just couldn't bear to live normally and going bush was the only thing he could think about doing, the only way he could cope with your rejection.'

By now, the tears were streaming down Rachel's face. 'Oh God, Pat, oh God, what shall I do? I love him to bits, and I caused all this, I was just angry and confused, if only he'd waited a few more days until I had calmed down.'

'It wasn't just you, the police force were pretty hard on him too and I think his wife, ex-wife was going to fight him over the children's access, something to do with them having a wonderful time with you I gather from what Mike said.'

They both sat quietly for a few moments then Rachel said, 'When were you going to tell me all this, Pat, were you ever?'

Pat nodded miserably. 'Yes, I thought if only I could make love to you, get you into my bed you'd be more inclined to think kindly of me, maybe let me stay on. Jesus, woman, you could do with some help around here!'

'That's why I'm selling, Pat, then I'm off to look for Mike, at least I've got a handle on where he is.'

'Don't hold your breath, me darlin', it was eight or nine weeks ago I saw Mike and I don't think he was going to hang around that long. He's gone bush, it becomes a way of life for some, so much so they can't settle down in the end.'

'Then the sooner I get a buyer for here the better.'

Pat nodded conceding that his plans were now a lost cause. Deep down, he knew it had been a long shot, but he'd had to try.

Pat stayed on for a bit helping Rachel out when he could, but they both knew his heart wasn't in it and it was time to part once again. Their friendship seemed to be on a different level, instead of feeling closer they both felt uncomfortable. Pat because he hadn't been honest and up front with

Rachel from the start and Rachel for the same reason but from a different perspective. So a couple of weeks later, Rachel wasn't surprised when at breakfast time Pat stuck his head round the door and said he was leaving shortly.

'I'm guessing you mean as in I won't be coming back?' Rachel asked.

'Aw, Rach, you know how I feel about you, it's hard, no, I need to move on, me darlin', understand?'

'Of course, Pat, I'm sorry to see you go, even Ruby will be sorry; you know you will always be welcome here as long as I'm here?'

Pat inclined his head then in a rush crossed the room and held Rachel tightly in his arms. 'Take care of yourself, me darlin' girl, I hope you find Mike the lucky bastard. I'll be ready to step into his shoes if he turns you down.'

Rachel hugged him back, her throat was too constricted to say much she just whispered, 'Take care Pat.' As he turned away, Rachel caught the hint of tears glistening in his eyes; then he was gone and seconds later, she heard the throaty roar of his motorbike

CHAPTER 54

Time marched on; it was a very hot summer and no rain. The paddocks were scorched, some of them turned to dust. Rachel got Sid and his men to help her move most of the cattle down to the furthest paddock where the creek seemed to be holding up well. Two of her bores had run nearly dry and what water there was, seemed brackish and salty. The winds blew hot and dry and dust got in everywhere, all the rooms in the house were covered in a film of dust in spite of the fact Rachel kept everything as closed up as possible. Record temperatures and still no rain. Greg told her it was very unlikely she would get a buyer unless it rained.

Sid was having to buy in feed, but Rachel was lucky as the bottom paddocks seemed to still have some feed; though, she decided she would have to cull some stock. She hadn't wanted to do this, but it seemed inevitable.

Rachel was sitting in her little office with the tower air conditioner going full blast when Greg rang. 'I can hardly believe it, Rachel, but I've had an enquiry about your place. I can't make out why anyone would be interested when we are in the middle of a drought. But anyway, the name I have is Macpherson, a Donald Macpherson and he wants to come out early next week and have a look around. Is that alright with you? Tuesday?'

Rachel's heart rate went up a notch. 'Yes that's fine Greg but you did stress that nothing looks that good didn't you?'

'Sure did; but he was adamant he wanted to come because I actually said to leave it for a couple of weeks in the hope it will look better if it rains.'

'Okay, well, Tuesday it is then, see you, Greg. Oh, yes, are you coming with him?'

'That was the plan, yes.'

When Rachel rang off, she sat for a while staring at the phone. She didn't know how she felt, pleased, sad, nervous, excited. Well this time next week he would have been and gone so she'd just have to wait and see what happened.

Sunday was even hotter, the mercury soared to 45 degrees then going outside to check the dog's water, Rachel smelt smoke. She stopped dead in her tracks, it was the thing everyone dreaded the most, a fire. Everything was tinder dry and if the wind got up it didn't bare thinking about. Turning on her heel, she went and got in the ute and drove to the highest point on her property, which was near the old homestead site. She looked to the east and could see a large column of smoke away on the horizon. However, it was a long way away and the winds were very light so she wouldn't panic yet she decided. Going back to the house, she rang Sid, Norma answered, 'Sid told me to ring you, Rach, but you beat me too it. Yes, the fire is over at old Nat Willerbys place. Don't know how it started but they are hoping it won't spread too far, there isn't much wind and they got onto it pretty quickly. Don't worry it's twenty or so k's away we should be alright.'

It was unsettling and before she went to bed that night, Rachel again got in the ute and drove up the hill. She could see a huge orange glow in the sky, but it didn't seem any nearer, as far as she could tell and feeling a little happier, she drove home and went to bed soon falling asleep.

Wind! Rachel jerked awake, it was blowing hard, she looked at the clock, 3am. Scrambling out of bed, she went through to the kitchen. Ruby, who slept out on the veranda scratched at the door, to be let in. As Rachel opened the door, the smell of smoke hit her, stronger, nearer, the wind was strong too and almost whipped the flyscreen door out of her hand.

With shaking hands, she got dressed, it brought back raw memories of the fire Johnny had started, thank goodness they had put it out quickly once Johnny and the gang were accounted for.

She could see the glow in the sky from the front veranda now but still got in the ute and drove up the hill. In the darkness, it was hard to see how near it was, but she could see it was much closer, and returning to the house checked her hoses then running the hose as far as she could, started to fill the gutters with water. A week before, she had blocked the down pipes in case this happened but had never really thought it would. Her water tanks were low, she had been saving water as much as she could, but the dry had gone on for some time, it was still getting low, in spite of her efforts. She got her large mobile water tank hitched to the ute then went inside to make herself a cup of tea, then she rang Norma.

Norma told her that the fire front was quite wide and it was heading towards town; however, there was a big cliff and scrubby land between the fire front and town and they were fairly confident they could stop it, but of course spot fires were the main risk. Sid was in the rural fire brigade, so he had gone off to help. 'The road will be a natural fire break, Rach, and they have a dozer they'll be making it wider if it comes closer. Try not to worry, there is a long day ahead of us as yet and they'll do all they can.'

'I know I'm sorry Norma, better get off the phone in case you're needed.' Rachel hung up. It was all very well but with no other human around, she couldn't stop worrying, she tried talking to Ruby who just wagged her tail. The sense of isolation swept over Rachel once again. If only there was someone to share this latest drama with her.

She spent the day driving up and down watching the fire, sometimes it seemed closer sometimes not but it wasn't so easy to see now as it was in the rough hilly country, which was just scrub land that as far as Rachel knew no one had ever bothered with. Then just before dark, it seemed to burst through into the scrub near her fence line. She was watching through binoculars so witnessed the fire suddenly erupting out of the bush where the land was flatter. It was now only about five kilometres away from where she stood and only a few hundred metres to her fence line. She jumped into the ute and rushed across the intervening paddocks as fast as she could. Ruby was leaning out of the open window, the wind blowing her ears back; she gave a little bark of excitement. 'Alright for you Ruby, but this is scary,' Rachel muttered through gritted teeth. Before she got near her fence line, she saw the first small fire burning in a small bushy area. It looked quite jolly in its way. Small flames dancing and whirling as if they were tiny people showing the world how to dance. Rachel telling Ruby to stay, was out of the truck with a shovel and beat the flames out. She didn't want to use the water bowser unless she had too. Then she saw another and another, the wind was whipping the embers from the main fire and dropping them onto the ground at Rachel's side, as she had guessed it would. If allowed to take hold, these little fires would soon become the roaring beast that was still some distance from the road and Rachel's boundary. As she worked rushing from one small upstart to another, she could hear the roar of the main fire and also the noise of the dozer that was desperately trying to make a firebreak the other side of the gravel road. Then quite suddenly there was a change, the atmosphere was different. Rachel stopped and looked around, the fire across the way was still burning but less fiercely, then Rachel realised that the wind had died down. She stood still savouring the change, would it last or was it just a lull. Finishing her task, she made her way back to the ute and an excited Ruby who had stayed as she was told, in the vehicle and drove cautiously to the fence line, looking for any smouldering embers on the way. As she parked, a figure tramped out of the gloom, the fire was still burning behind him, so he was only a silhouette and until he spoke Rachel didn't realise it was Greg. All bluster was gone, and he gave Rachel a grin. His teeth looked so white against his blackened face.

'Should be okay now, Rachel, so long as the wind doesn't get up again. We've back burned and made large fire breaks, so hopefully we'll be right. It quite often drops at sunset, you okay?'

'Yea, relieved I guess, lucky or what?'

Greg turned away then turned back again. 'Got Maisie to put that bloke on hold for a day or two what with the fire and all.'

'Thanks, yes, I don't feel ready for a viewing tomorrow that's for sure.'

Rachel drove home feeling so dog tired all she wanted to do was feed the dogs, shower and climb into bed. Thank goodness, she had a few days respite before she had to face this Macpherson person. She half woke in the night to hear rain drumming on the roof; she turned over with a sigh of relief.

CHAPTER 55

The next morning Rachel dragged herself out of bed, her eyes were sore from the smoke yesterday and were not focussing very well, her limbs felt leaden. Ruby was quiet too. Not bothering to get dressed, Rachel padded into the kitchen in an old tea shirt she slept in, her hair was a mess, she had washed it before bed but to her she still smelt of smoke. Yawning she put the coffee on and slumped down at the table. Ruby lifted her head and gave a low growl. Moments later, Rachel heard a vehicle pull up. Snatching an old coat from the pegs in the hall, Rachel opened the front door.

'Must be that Macpherson bloke, Ruby,' she said to the dog, 'didn't he get the message, well; he will just have to come back another day.'

It looked like a very new four by four, and was close to the veranda steps. Rachel's eyes didn't seem to be very clear and the man getting out looked familiar. Rachel's legs all at once felt weak, she was seeing things, she must be, was it Mike? It was, it was Mike. He bounded up the steps and his arms were around her; his lips were on hers, she felt faint and almost slipped to the floor, but he held her up.

'Whoa, steady on, darlin', you okay?' He guided her onto the little cane sofa that was just there.

Rachel couldn't speak with swimming eyes she looked at him and stroked his dear face with her hand nodding as she did so. Mike took her hand and pressed a kiss on her palm. Ruby didn't like being left out and pushed her head between them, Rachel laughed then and managed to say, 'Where did you come from, oh, Mike, I am so sorry, the things I said. I didn't mean them. I love you. I—'

Mike stopped her with a deep kiss then standing up, lifted her in his arms and carried her indoors to the bedroom. He peeled the old coat off and her tea shirt then laid her on the bed, telling her not to talk as she opened her mouth to speak. Rachel lay quietly as he explored her body with knowing hands and lips, then Rachel could lie back no longer and was helping Mike out of his clothes with as much haste as she could, pulling him into her frantically. Mike tried to hold back, but they climaxed together and finally, both lay side by side temporarily spent.

Rachel sat up suddenly. 'I put the coffee on, but I don't remember if it's got enough water in it.' She scrambled up and ran into the kitchen, it was fine but wouldn't have been much longer. Then the phone rang. Rachel snatched up, who could that be? It was Maisie. 'I'm so sorry, Mrs Conway, but Mr Macpherson was insistent he would still come out to your place this morning I couldn't persuade him not to.'

'Oh Hell, Maisie. Okay, well don't worry I'll deal with him when he gets here.'

'Thanks, Mrs Conway. I'm sorry.'

'No worries, bye, Maisie.'

Rachel turned around straight into Mike's arms, he just come up behind her, they were both still naked and she could feel Mike's desire was returning; but she pushed him away gently.

'There is some man on his way out here, Mike, I'd better get dressed. He wants to buy this place. I put it up for sale a while ago; he's the first to show any interest. Greg had told Maisie to tell him not to come today, but he obviously didn't get the message.'

'I don't think you should get dressed for him; you look good as you are; what man could resist you?' Mike was grinning from ear to ear as he said this.

Rachel looked at him puzzled for a heartbeat then said, 'Are you this Macpherson bloke?'

Taking her hand, Mike nodded then led her into the kitchen and set about pouring coffee and putting toast on, talking as he did so.

'You've rumbled me, Rach, yes, it's me. It was my uncle's surname; but there is a lot more to it than me just coming to see you. First of all, if you want to leave, not live here with me or not be with me at all, then I will buy you out.' At this stage, Mike put his hand up as Rachel went to speak. 'Hear me out, Rach, please. I love you more than I ever thought possible to love anyone and because of that I fucked up our relationship and my career, but you know all that. When you were so angry I understood to start with, but I thought you would come round, but it seemed as if I made a big mistake and maybe you didn't love me; not enough anyway. I hit rock bottom, Rach, and decided to go bush. I didn't want to see anyone I knew or have anything to do with anyone at all. I met Patrick by chance and told him everything that had happened, and he told me I was a fool. A fool to give up so easily with you and a fool to cut myself off from my family. He wished he'd stayed more in touch with Shawn, it's something he really regrets. So, having thought about it for a while, I rang home and found out that my mother was in hospital and they were all very worried about her. So, I hightailed it home. Mum has recovered, but here is the weird bit. Mum had a twin brother, an identical twin and he died at the same time Mum fell ill.' Mike stopped for a moment and took a big gulp of coffee; Rachel waited not knowing what was coming next.

'Two things happened then, one was I found out you'd been looking for me, oh, Rach, I couldn't believe it, then I found out my uncle had left me his entire estate. He figured that everyone else had land and cattle and he knew it was deep inside me, in my blood, whatever you like to call it. So he left me enough to start out on my own. He was a miner and we all thought he was a dreamer; not well off at all. He never married, was just obsessed with looking for the 'Big One' as he used to say. We never saw much of him, but he was a lot better off than any of us knew.'

The telephone rang again; they looked at each other. 'I'd better answer it, it might be important,' Rachel got to her feet.

'Hello, Rachel, Norma here. How are you, love, are you okay?'

Rachel found herself wanting to sing and laugh and cry all at once but managed to say, 'I am, Norma, I am.'

'You sound odd, Rachel, are you sure?'

'Yes, yes, I'm sure, look Norma I'm a little busy can I call you back later?'

Mike had pulled on a pair of shorts while she was talking to Norma and was once again sitting at the table but looking rather uneasy.

'What is your answer, Rachel; can we be partners here, invest in making this the best Brahman stud in Queensland or would you rather I just leave again; or what do you think?'

'Mike, need you ask, I love you too, you might have to look out for me when I'm in my wheel chair, but yes, please. Oh, Mike, please don't leave me again, ever.'

EPILOGUE

It was going to be a very hot day; Rachel looked across the paddocks, which were dotted with cattle whose glossy hides seemed to almost glow in the early morning sun. Just then, two excited children came flying in the back door, followed by their father. 'Daddy says we can name the new little chicks that are just hatched, Rachel, but Em says that's silly. They're just chooks!' Ben looked at his sister mutinously.

'Well, you can give them names. Em doesn't have to call them by those names if she doesn't want to, does she?'

'No, s'pose not, what's for breakfast?'

'How about pancakes with bacon and maple syrup?'

Both children cheered then Em put her arms round Rachel's hips, as high as she could reach. 'Love you, Rach,' she said.

'I second that,' said Mike.

Rachel was smiling widely as she made the batter for the pancakes. She wasn't alone any longer. She had Mike of course and during the holidays, she had two delightful children as well. Being alone was well in the past and she hoped it would never be in the future.

ALONE

Gillian Wells
Visit my website at www.Gillianwellsauthor.com.au

Shawline Publishing Group Pty Ltd
www.shawlinepublishing.com.au

SHAWLINE
PUBLISHING
GROUP

CPSIA information can be obtained
at www.ICGtesting.com
Printed in the USA
LVHW031923071120
671047LV00007B/683

9 781922 444134